E?

There is no greater voice in defense of the lives of the unborn than the voices of the women (and men) who aborted their own child. The lies that defend or promote abortion are clearly made obvious through the terrible suffering of countless women and men who are "victims" of abortion by the decision they once made to end the life of their unborn child.

Theresa Bonopartis speaks from her heart of her journey into the Heart of Christ where, at last, she found healing and peace. It is a journey that offers hope, not only to individual men and women who endure the painful consequences of their decision, but also to our contemporary culture that seems to have lost its way.

A Journey to Healing Through Divine Mercy is certainly a must-read. The meditations that Theresa Bonopartis provides for us are a reminder of the words of Pope Francis: "We are all sinners, but God heals us with an abundance of grace, mercy, and tenderness."

May we all journey into the Heart of Christ, into an experience of Divine Mercy.

—Rev. Mariusz Koch, CFR

Theresa Bonopartis speaks as one who truly understands the transforming power of Divine Mercy for those of us who have been touched by the pain of abortion and desire healing that can restore wholeness. Throughout these moving reflections, one is gently led on a private journey through the healing process and offered hope for reconciliation and eventual restoration.

These thoughtful meditations speak to the heart of anyone who has shared in the painful experience of what it is to be impacted by abortion and the devastation and silence that often follows. The process of healing is complex, different for everyone, and a journey that requires faith, which may seem to be lost.

With excerpts from St. Faustina's *Diary* and affirmations from popes, Theresa allows the reader to trust in the process of mercy even with the trials of temptation, fear, and the ability to forgive and accept forgiveness. She offers reflections on her own personal struggles, yet brings with her the wisdom of many years working in God's ministry of offering others a way to healing through His love and mercy. She uncovers many of the feelings and conflicts so many of us deal with, even years after this loss in our lives.

—Mary Kominski — Catholic campus minister, post-abortion speaker, and group facilitator

Over the past 25 years of working with women and men who have experienced the pain of a past abortion, I have marveled at God's mercy manifested in their lives. Understanding His mercy intellectually is one thing; experiencing it in such a palpable way is quite another. Seeing lives transformed by this relationship with Mercy Himself is a humbling thing to witness. If I had ever doubted God's love and mercy, those doubts would be shattered by the witness of so many that I've seen go from the depths of despair to the true and tangible joy of living in His light. My heart leaps with joy to know the blessings God has in store for those who turn humbly to His mercy. Theresa's book will be a great companion, whether one has experienced an abortion or not. It's a message and witness for all of us sinners that God's Mercy triumphs even over the worst and most painful of sins. I pray that countless souls will be drawn to His beautiful Mercy. May His Holy Name be praised and glorified forever.

— Allison Ricciardi, LMHC — founder, CatholicTherapists.com

We are all sinners. And God knows what we all need: Divine Mercy. And this He offers us through Christ, the incarnation of Divine Mercy, a mercy so great that even though we have rejected Him, betrayed Him, persecuted and crucified Him, He *still rises up* to offer us His Mercy again and again.

To experience Divine Mercy, especially after honestly confronting our many faults, is both humbling and exalting. It is life-changing, soul-altering, and a gift that must be shared with others.

Theresa Bonopartis' booklet is an excellent guide to deepening one's understanding and experience of Divine Mercy. It draws on her own personal experience of the life-transforming power of Christ's healing mercy and her daily ministry in sharing Divine Mercy with those who have languished in despair.

A Journey to Healing Through Divine Mercy is a wonderful guide for contemplation that deepens your own healing and experience with mercy while also aiding you to share Divine Mercy with others.

— David Reardon, PhD, founder, The Elliot Institute

A Journey to Healing

Through Divine Mercy

MERCY AFTER ABORTION

Theresa Bonopartis

MARIAN PRESS
STOCKBRIDGE · MA 01263

2016

Available from:
Marian Helpers Center
Stockbridge, MA 01263
1-800-462-7426
marian.org
ShopMercy.org

Library of Congress Control Number: 2016916860
ISBN: 978-1-59614-369-2

Imprimi Potest:
Very Rev. Kazimierz Chwalek, MIC
Provincial Superior
The Blessed Virgin Mary, Mother of Mercy Province
July 30, 2016

Nihil Obstat:
Dr. Robert A. Stackpole, STD
Censor Deputatus
July 30, 2016

All papal texts © Libreria Editrice Vaticana

Note on quotes from the *Diary of Saint Maria Faustina Kowalska*:
Bold text indicates the words of Jesus or God the Father;
italicized text indicates the words of the Blessed Virgin Mary.

Printed in the United States of America

This is the time for mercy. It is the favorable time to heal wounds, a time not to be weary of meeting all those who are waiting to see and to touch with their hands the signs of the closeness of God, a time to offer everyone the way of forgiveness and reconciliation.

—**Pope Francis, Homily,
First Vespers of Divine Mercy Sunday, 2015**

I would now like to say a special word to women who have had an abortion. The Church is aware of the many factors which may have influenced your decision, and she does not doubt that in many cases it was a painful and even shattering decision. The wound in your heart may not yet have healed. Certainly what happened was and remains terribly wrong. But do not give in to discouragement and do not lose hope. Try rather to understand what happened and face it honestly. If you have not already done so, give yourselves over with humility and trust to repentance. The Father of mercies is ready to give you his forgiveness and his peace in the Sacrament of Reconciliation. To the same Father and his mercy you can with sure hope entrust your child. With the friendly and expert help and advice of other people, and as a result of your own painful experience, you can be among the most eloquent defenders of everyone's right to life.

—**St. John Paul II,
Encyclical Letter *Evangelium Vitae*, 99**

Table of Contents

Preface

I would like to begin with a little story:

In 2002, the United States Conference of Catholic Bishops (USCCB) asked me to put my testimony down on paper so that they could include it in their yearly Respect Life Month packet to be distributed to all parishes throughout the United States. Since I had been tormented by the experience of a past abortion and healed by Divine Mercy, and since I also wanted to spread the message of God's mercy, I was more than happy to do so. (See Part One for my testimony.)

Once the packets were printed, I was sent a box. I will never forget my mortification when I opened it up. There before me was my testimony with the title "Divine Mercy in My Soul," the same title that the *Diary* of St. Faustina has!

I love St. Faustina's *Diary* and read it often. This saint of mercy was so pure and holy! I could not believe they had given the witness of my life, so totally different from St. Faustina's, the same name as her *Diary*! I was completely mortified and began panicking. This was going to be all over the country! What would people think?

Not knowing what to do, I quickly called my spiritual director. Thinking he would advise me about how to fix this, I made an appointment to see him. However, he gave me a completely different response than the one I had hoped for. "Theresa," he said to me, "it is 'Divine Mercy In Your Soul.' Accept the title in humility, for your story is not about you, but about the love and mercy of God."

God works in each of us in different ways according to our needs, but it is His mercy *in each one of our souls* that brings us all to *Him*, no matter our experiences. This book of reflections was created as a way for you to personally experience Mercy Himself. It is my hope that it will assist in freeing you from the grief, sorrow, guilt, and shame of abortion, and bring you consolation and reconciliation with God, your child, and yourself.

Inspired by the Jubilee Year of Mercy, I put together this book of reflections as a way to help you have your own personal experience of Jubilee, of being set free from the weight of your sins, of being allowed to rest from grief and sorrow, of a year of liberty and reconciliation with God, your neighbor, and yourself. Thus, the meditations are divided up by the seasons of the year. Read them in those seasons or read them all at your own pace; it's up to you and your guardian angel. This book is meant to bring the Jubilee Year experience into each and every year, for we are in the time of mercy, and Jesus wants us all to be set free. And so, I dedicate this book to each of you, knowing that Jesus, who is Mercy Himself, is waiting for you, longing to set you free!

Part One

'Divine Mercy in My Soul':
My Witness to Divine Mercy

JESUS I TRUST IN YOU

"We are to show to those in need His goodness to ourselves … ."

This phrase at Mass speaks to my heart. It reminds me of the despair, the grief, the pain of abortion from which Christ delivered me. It reminds me also of my duty to give hope to those still suffering, to help point the way to a place of shelter and peace in the Heart of Jesus. And so, I relate my experience — unique and personal, but not unlike the stories of many other women. But this story is not, finally, about me. It's about our good and merciful God ... always there, wanting to forgive us and to make us whole again.

At 18, I honestly believed I was the only one not having sex. I gave in to peer pressure and slept with someone I was seeing occasionally. I remember vividly the day I phoned the doctor for my test results and learned I was pregnant.

After months of denial, I was nearly four months pregnant, so I knew the answer long before the word "positive" was uttered. I was overwhelmed by a range of feelings: happiness at the thought of a child growing within me, but also fear of telling my parents — the reason I had "denied" it for so long.

I immediately told the father of the child, and we decided to get married. Although we planned to tell our parents together, I blurted out the truth to my mother and father. Their reaction took me by surprise. Shocked, angry, and disappointed, they told me to leave the house and forget that I was their daughter.

In retrospect, their reaction was understandable. They believed that premarital sex was wrong and thought it would be a disgrace to have a child out of wedlock. At least, I thought, my parents were practicing Catholics and would never ask me to abort my child. I left the house with no job, no money, no home, and nowhere to turn, feeling utterly abandoned and alone. It wasn't long before the baby's father and I broke up. Still, I was certain I would not get an abortion. I wanted my child.

A friend's mother invited me to stay in their home. I had no idea how I could support the baby and myself, and things began to feel hopeless. During this period, my father sent several messages urging me to have an abortion. He even offered to pay for it. I refused. But as I began to feel more desperate, I decided, finally, to let the abortion happen. I shut down my feelings and went through the motions, functioning more like an observer in a surreal world than someone in control.

Thirty years later, I still can't remember how I got to the hospital. But I do remember being alone in the hospital room when a doctor entered, and I'll never forget the sadistic look on his face as he injected saline into my abdomen.

No one explained to me the baby's development or what the abortion would be like. I had no idea what was going to happen. I lay there just wishing that I could die. I could feel the baby thrashing around as his skin and lungs were burned by the saline. He was dying. Labor began. After 12 hours of labor, alone in the room, I gave birth to a dead baby boy.

I looked at his tiny feet and hands. All I wanted to do was to pick up my son and put him back inside of me. I couldn't fathom what I had done. I rang for the nurse. She came in, picked up my son and dumped him in what looked like a large mayonnaise jar, a jar marked "3A." Then she left the room and I was alone again, filled with hatred for myself. The thought of death seemed comforting. My downward spiral had only just begun.

After the abortion, I flew to California to spend time with my sister and her family so I could get my bearings again. I wasn't the same person anymore. I went through the motions of daily living, but I had no desire for anything. At night, in the room I shared with my 2-year-old niece, I'd lie awake asking God over and over again to forgive me.

Three months later, I returned to the New York area. Although I was not in contact with my father, my mom would slip out to meet me occasionally. Still trying to run away from myself, I moved to Florida. During my two years there, I called my dad and we began speaking again, although never mentioning my abortion.

When I returned to the area, I found a job, and outwardly, things seemed fine. But nothing was as it seemed. I tried hard not to think about who I was and what I had done. When I thought about my dead child, I would become depressed and despairing. Desperate to be loved, I became involved with the man I would marry, even though he was emotionally and psychologically abusive to me.

Two years later, I was thrilled to be pregnant with our first child. But I was also afraid that God would punish me for the abortion, that something would be wrong with my child. I prayed constantly that the baby would not have to suffer for my sins, and was immensely relieved when he was born healthy.

The marriage began to fall apart soon after the baby's birth. My husband was abusing alcohol and we were arguing all the time. We tried counseling to salvage our marriage. Knowing that my abortion was at the root of my problems, I told the counselor about it. He told me to just forget about it. It was in the past. I could not make him understand that the abortion was very much in the present because I was living with the consequences every day.

For a while, my husband stayed sober, and I became pregnant with our second child. By the time I was to give birth, however, his addiction was again full-blown. The night our second child was born, I did not expect my husband to be there. By the time he got home, I was well along in labor and we barely made it to the hospital in time.

The birth of my son was anything but joyous. I didn't know how I was going to care for two children, living with someone addicted to alcohol. Unlike the husbands of mothers around me, my husband did not show up the next day; he was recovering from a hangover. I lay alone in a hospital room, but this time my child was alive.

Soon after I brought the baby home, my husband overdosed and had to be rushed to the hospital. The incident helped me to begin breaking the cycle. During his two-week hospital stay, I began to enjoy my children for the first time. I didn't have to worry about where he was or what he was doing. I gave the children my full attention. I promised myself that I would not let them grow up in an abusive home, and that if he didn't straighten out, the children and I would begin a life for ourselves.

I kept my sanity by praying and reading the Bible. My husband stayed sober for two years before it began all over again. The day my older son, then 4, told me to hide in the closet when he saw his father coming home, I knew we would have to leave.

For myself, I might well have stayed in that abusive relationship forever, but I did not want the boys to experience abuse. One day when my husband was drinking again, I took the children and walked out the door. Once again, I found myself with no job, no money, no home. This time, thank God, I had my children.

My sister took me in to her already full apartment, and with my family's help (in this crisis I had their full support), I began to get my life together. Shortly after I walked out, my husband ended up in rehab, so the boys and I were able to move back into our apartment. I found a job. Within a year or two, I returned to school to train as a substance abuse counselor. My family helped me both financially and by helping to care for the boys. I could not have made it without them.

After graduation, one of my teachers offered me a job. I thought I had finally gotten it together. Little did I realize how fragile this new life was.

By this time, I had grown in my spiritual life and had a relationship with God, even though I did not truly know Him and still kept a distance from church. I still suffered from depression, entertained thoughts of suicide and had very low self-esteem; the fact that I had been one of the few from my class to be offered a job did not raise my self-esteem.

In time, as I struggled with my personal problems, my professional work began to suffer. I experienced burn out. It was devastating to have worked so hard to achieve what I had and then become unable to function. I realize now that it was God's way of drawing me closer to Him.

I quit my job and struggled to stay out of the hospital. My dad supported the kids and me. I just moved through life. Every day it was a challenge just to get out of bed and take care of the boys. I did, however, begin attending Mass again, sitting in the back of the church, certain that everyone knew I had had an abortion, certain that the walls would come crashing down on me. But I went, listening for some word of hope that I could be forgiven for my terrible, "unforgivable" sin.

By then my older son was 7 and ready to make his First Penance. At a meeting for the parents, a priest talked about God's mercy and His desire to forgive any sin, even the sin of abortion. I remember thinking: "Can this be true? Did I hear him correctly? Will God really forgive abortion?" That evening I left with the first inkling of hope I had known in 10 years.

It took time and courage, but I decided to contact that priest and ask him to hear my confession. Scared and nervous, I made my first confession in many years. The priest was gentle, trying to make it as easy as he could for me. He showed great empathy and support. At last, I was on my way home.

I began to see the priest regularly for spiritual direction. At first, all I could see was darkness. It was an effort to do the things he asked, like examining my life, because I was sure I would uncover only what a terrible person I was. But I was tired of depression and desperate enough to try. I felt sorry for my children who had a mom who cried a lot and simply couldn't cope with life. I wanted more for the three of us. And so I prayed, went to Mass every day, and spent time before the Blessed Sacrament. I needed so badly to trust in this God I had been told was so good.

Still I could not forgive myself. I continued to struggle with depression. I would beg Jesus for healing. I felt bad that I had not reached full healing, and my confessor's eyes showed his own sadness over my continued struggle. I understand now that the fullness of healing must come in God's time.

One night I felt depressed and suicidal again, but despite these feelings, I also somehow felt a deep trust in God. I didn't want the children to see me crying again, so after putting them to bed, I closed myself in the bathroom, crouched on the floor, and repeated over and over, "Jesus, I trust in You."

I don't know how many hours I did this, but well into the night, I had an experience that changed my life. I experienced being on the Cross with Christ. But instead of experiencing suffering, I felt love so intense that it was capable of taking away that pain. I felt His love wash away my sin and I knew my healing was complete.

I have never since felt the despair of abortion, only the profound love and forgiveness Christ gave me. I've watched my life be transformed, miraculously, as I've been privileged to help countless women and men suffering from abortion's aftermath. Christ's love transformed not only my life, but also the lives of those I love.

Before my mother died, I learned that my abortion had caused her great suffering, although she had never told me. One day when we were watching TV, abortion was mentioned. She said, "Well, sometimes it's all right to have an abortion." I said, "Mom, it is never all right."

God gave us this moment of grace. Mom told me that my abortion was her sin and that she would take it to the grave with her. I was able to comfort her, telling her that we both bore responsibility for it. I told her that I forgave her and asked her to forgive me. After that, my mother went to Confession to the same priest I had seen for direction, and she felt that her terrible burden was lifted.

Most difficult was telling my children. I felt that God was calling me to speak out about abortion, but I knew I couldn't unless my children knew first. I was terrified they would hate me. It took me years to muster the courage. By now, I was active in the pro-life movement and they had been brought up to respect human life.

I planned to tell them many times, but each time I backed out, afraid to say the words. Finally, one day I knew I was being given the grace to talk to them. How can I describe that day? I trembled as I told them of how our lives had come to be as they were. If not for my abortion, they would not be living in a fatherless household or seeing the strained relationship between my father and me.

The boys wrestled with their feelings. They were angry at me. They grieved for the brother they never knew. They felt guilty for surviving. It took time, a lot of talking, and the grace of God, but they understood finally why things were as they were, and why I had spent years crying. They grew closer to God, and we grew closer to one another.

I didn't speak publicly right away. The boys needed time to deal with their feelings and cope with the loss of their brother before I would do that. I was even resigned and at peace with the fact that the day might never come. But a few years later, they gave me their blessing. To say I am proud of them is an understatement. They have become great advocates for life.

I have now worked for many years in a post-abortion ministry I developed with the Sisters of Life, *Entering Canaan: A Sacramental Journey to an Inheritance of Mercy*. Since its inception, the ministry has, with the help of the Franciscan Friars of the Renewal, grown to include a track for men and one for siblings. I am grateful to be able to stand at the foot of the Cross with those who come, and blessed to watch them be transformed by God's love and forgiveness. I have witnessed countless miracles of His mercy and am convinced that God is marshaling an army of once-wounded women and men to dispel the lies of abortion.

The *Diary of Saint Maria Faustina Kowalska: Divine Mercy in My Soul* tells of words spoken to her by Christ:

> **Let the greatest sinners place their trust in My mercy. They have the right before others to trust in the abyss of My mercy. My daughter, write about My mercy towards tormented souls. Souls that make an appeal to My mercy delight Me. To such souls I grant even more graces than asked. I cannot punish even the greatest sinner if he makes an appeal to My compassion, but on the contrary, I justify him in My unfathomable and inscrutable mercy.**

I know that this is true.

Jesus, I trust in You!

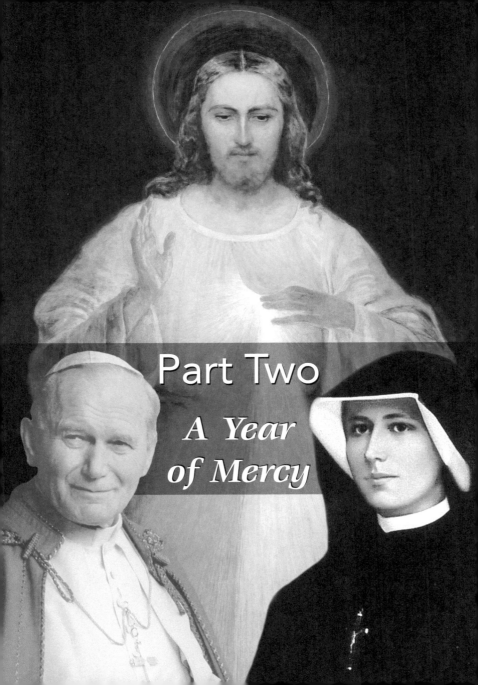

Part Two

A *Year* of Mercy

Winter

Tell [all people], **My daughter, that I am Love and Mercy itself. When a soul approaches Me with trust, I fill it with such an abundance of graces that it cannot contain them within itself, but radiates them to other souls.**

— *Diary*, 1074

Because of His Mercy

Because of my conversion, a painfully quiet, shy person has turned into someone who has plenty to say. Why? Because my trust is in the Lord and not myself. He took the worst sin of my life and brought good out of it. In the aftermath of my horrific sin of abortion, He showed me the immense love and mercy He has, not only for me, but also for all sinners. What a gift for someone who deserves nothing but condemnation!

It is because of this experience of limitless mercy shown to me in the face of such a terrible sin that I was able to repent. To look at my sin before then would have been impossible. It was just too horrific. *I did not repent before His mercy; I repented because of His mercy.*

When faced with the gravity of [Adam and Eve's] sin, God responds with the fullness of mercy ... Mercy will always be greater than any sin, and no one can place limits on the love of God who is ever ready to forgive.

— Pope Francis, announcement of the extraordinary Jubilee Year of Mercy, St. Peter's Basilica, March 13, 2015

My daughter, at God's command I am to be, in a special and exclusive way, your Mother; but I desire that you, too, in a special way, be My child.

— *Diary*, 1414

Clinging to 'Us'
December 8
Solemnity of the Immaculate Conception

It is amazing how we cling to all that is "us." With every ounce of our being, we build a fortress of "self" to supposedly shield us from harm. The trouble is that, most times, it also shields us from joy, leaving us unable to truly love and live in the present moment with God.

We are not born with this shield. Our human nature trusted our parents to provide for all of our needs when we were infants. It is through our disappointments from others and the pain that we have experienced that we erect the wall of (what we falsely believe is) protection.

On this Solemnity of the Immaculate Conception, I cannot help but reflect upon the ability of Mary to remain open in spite of the disappointments and pain she experienced. In her complete surrender to God, she accepted what He allowed in her life because she completely believed in Him and His love for her, no matter how things seemed. That is a hard thing to accomplish, and impossible without His grace.

From the Annunciation of the Lord to the journey to the stable in Bethlehem, she trusted, even though, in human terms, it would appear that God had abandoned her.

Even as she fled in the night with Joseph; learned about the slaughter of the Holy Innocents; stood in front of the house of Pilate, hearing shouts of "crucify Him"; walked to Calvary and beheld the death of her Son; even through all of that, Mary continued to love, building no shield and allowing nothing to separate her from God's love — not even indescribable pain.

As we celebrate the Solemnity of the Immaculate Conception, may each one of us learn to cling, not to ourselves or to other mere mortals, but like Mary, to Jesus Christ alone, Mercy Himself, who brings us joy and salvation.

> In the "fullness of time" (Gal 4:4), when everything had been arranged according to his plan of salvation, he sent his only Son into the world, born of the Virgin Mary, to reveal his love for us in a definitive way. Whoever sees Jesus sees the Father (cf. Jn 14:9). Jesus of Nazareth, by his words, his actions, and his entire person reveals the mercy of God.
>
> — Pope Francis, *Misericordiae Vultus*, Bull of Indiction of the Extraordinary Jubilee of Mercy, 1

Write down these words, My daughter, Speak to the world about My mercy; let all mankind recognize My unfathomable mercy. It is a sign for the end times; after it will come the day of justice.

— *Diary*, 848

Mercy, So Great a Gift

There was a blog post by Msgr. Charles Pope on the Archdiocese of Washington website a while ago, titled "Mercy! So Great a Gift — Why Many Parishes Need to Reconsider When They Offer the Sacrament of Confession."

In this beautiful article, Msgr. Pope tells the story of St. John Paul II and a bishop who resigned because he fell from grace by having an affair with a woman. Following his resignation, the Pope asked to see him:

> The bishop was apprehensive, not knowing what to expect. He had let the Holy Father and God's people down and a thousand nervous thoughts rushed through his mind. As he drew close, Pope John Paul II extended his large, muscular arms and put a hand on each shoulder of the bishop. He looked him in the eye and said, "Are you at peace?" Relief and a profound sense of mercy flooded the bishop's heart; his eyes often filled with tears as he recounted the story years later.

> There is perhaps no greater gift than to experience the power and beauty of mercy. Yet it is a gift that is often wrapped in pain and in the humiliation of

having experienced the true weight of our sins. It is no accident that the opening words of our Lord's proclamation were "Repent and believe the good news" (Mk 1:15), specifically in that order. For unless we know the bad news, the good news is no news. To repent is to come to a new mind that, beholding God's glory and holiness, sees the need for mercy. But oh, the glory then of the good news: mercy is available in abundance! God will never reject anyone who calls on Him (Jn 6:37). Oh, the relief, the peace of knowing the effect of those words spoken by God through His priests: "I absolve you from your sins ... go in peace."

When I read this account of the bishop experiencing the mercy of God, I knew exactly what he was feeling: that intimate encounter with our God of Mercy that touches our very soul.

Like this bishop, I had also been wrapped in humiliation because of the weight of my sin — in my case, the sin of abortion. I, too, had cried out for God's mercy as I sat on the floor of my bathroom one night over 20 years ago, immersed in the agony of my sin, repeating over and over again as I crouched on the floor, "Jesus, I trust in You!"

My experience was one of surrender, climbing on the Cross of Christ to find there, not pain, but His immense love and mercy. A rush of warmth went through me, and I immediately knew that I had been healed.

It is hard to describe this experience. There are no words to adequately express that encounter with God's mercy, but it is a moment that you carry with you forever. That moment sustains you through many trials because you know you have met Mercy Himself.

Mercy: the bridge that connects God and man, opening our hearts to the hope of being loved forever despite our sinfulness.

— Pope Francis, *Misericordiae Vultus*, Bull of Indiction of the Extraordinary Jubilee of Mercy

And I understood that the greatest attribute is love and mercy. It unites the creature with the Creator. This immense love and abyss of mercy are made known in the Incarnation of the Word and in the Redemption [of humanity], and it is here that I saw this as the greatest of all God's attributes.

— *Diary*, 180

The Birth of Mercy
(Being post-abortive in the Advent and Christmas seasons)

I can still remember it as if it were yesterday: making Christmas stockings for my nieces and nephews the Christmas immediately following my abortion. That was over 40 years ago, and yet I remember those stockings vividly: the materials, the images, the pain of sewing them together as I thought of my son, who would be missing from the Christmas celebration.

That agonizing pain did not leave as the years went on, although I must admit I fell into such deep denial that I was not aware that my lack of joy was a consequence of my abortion. Society did not acknowledge my pain and grief. So in order to survive, I pressed my feelings into the recesses of my mind and, like everyone else, denied their existence.

Over the years, no matter what my situation in life, Christmas was a time of turmoil, a dreaded event, even after the birth of my other children. Many Christmas Eves were spent crying as I prepared presents, not really understanding why I was feeling the way I was. This was supposed to be a time filled with joyful expectation, but I was anything but joyful.

When I finally found someone to help me through my healing process, I began to see the reason for my sadness, and everything began to make sense. My "no" to life became magnified by Mary's "yes." I also was all too aware of the absence of toys for my aborted son, toys that would never be brought by Santa and placed under our tree. The emptiness of his space at the family holiday table seemed to scream at me. There was no room for the birth of Jesus in the stable of my heart, which was deadened because of my sin.

In time, through counseling, prayer, and a great spiritual director, I learned to take my eyes off *me* at Christmas and instead turn my gaze to *Him*: Jesus Christ. As healing came, I meditated on the mystery of the Incarnation instead of thinking about my abortion. Rather than focusing on who was missing, I turned my gaze to who was here: Mercy Himself, who came to earth for our salvation!

Instead of remaining a dreaded holiday for me, Christmas came to mean the opening chapter of the means of my salvation. God came to earth as an infant to take our sins — even my sin of abortion — upon Himself so that we could be saved. Mercy Himself was born into the world, and through His life, Death, and Resurrection, the gates of Heaven were opened to repentant sinners.

There have been close to 60 million abortions in the United States since 1973. As the Catholic bishops call for increased outreach to those who are post-abortive, let us be ever mindful of the countless women and men who have not yet found healing and, with St. Faustina, proclaim to them, "How great is the mercy of God contained in the Mystery of the Incarnation of the Son of God!" (*Diary*, 1433).

Jesus, we trust in You!

> In this way, God shows that He is merciful towards humanity, and filled with love for us. He is God-with-us: do you believe this?

> — Pope Francis, General Audience,
> December 18, 2013

Today I have fought a battle with the spirits of darkness over one soul. How terribly Satan hates God's mercy! I see how he opposes this whole work!

— *Diary*, 812

The Walk of Faith in Healing

Suppose someone tells you that you must walk through a tunnel of darkness in order to come to the light of life on the other side. It is a matter of life and death. The only other option will be to live in pain with no escape.

You will not be able to sense anyone walking through it with you, but you are promised a person will accompany you and be at your disposal. You will be able to speak to him, and he will help you combat any obstacles you may face. It will take a lot of trust in that person's love and care for you to begin the journey. Maybe you do not know that person well; perhaps you have heard of him and know that he has aided others, but you have no personal relationship with him.

So how do you trust? One step at a time. As you slowly move through the darkness and learn at each step that the person can be trusted, you begin to trust more as you take the next step and the next. Soon, even though you know you are walking through danger, you come to believe that, with the help of that unseen friend, you will come out the other side safely.

Walking in a tunnel of darkness is a difficult thing for anyone. Our senses are barely helpful and we seem to have no control over our fate. Every step is full of fear. We are afraid of the possibility that we might be in danger. We don't know what is before us. We imagine all the threats we are most afraid of creeping up on us and destroying us. There may be something ahead that will cause us to fall, or even more frightening, there may be ghosts from our past lurking in the darkness, waiting to do us harm.

This walk is especially difficult for those post-abortive men and women who have often experienced complete isolation and abandonment. It takes a courage born out of desperation, a belief that it is worth the risk in order to come to the end of the pain to even set out on the journey, let alone complete it. We must have trust in the merciful love of Jesus Christ, our Savior and guide throughout the journey.

It is frightening, but what is the alternative? Do we proceed along the path toward the light in faith and trust, or do we choose to live out our lives in the pain and agony we have been experiencing? To remain as we are would be to live our lives without love. Take a risk, one step at a time … He will not abandon you!

> The Lord is good and his faithfulness never abandons us because he is always ready to sustain us with his merciful love. With this confidence, the psalmist yields to God's embrace: "Learn to savor how good the Lord is"
>
> — Pope John Paul II, General Audience,
> January 8, 2003

My sanctity and perfection consist in the close union of my will with the will of God. God never violates our free will. It is up to us whether we want to receive God's grace or not. It is up to us whether we will cooperate with it or waste it.

— *Diary*, 1107

Refusing God's Forgiveness

I have met people who refused to accept God's forgiveness. Sounds crazy, I know. Who would not want God's forgiveness? But some people truly just want to continue punishing themselves. They think that by continually beating themselves up, they will somehow make up for their abortion. It reminds me of a scene in the movie "The Mission," where one of the characters drags a bundle of armor and weaponry up the mountain as penance for his sins. It takes him forever to trust enough to let his burden go and accept God's love.

We can become comfortable even in our unhealthy behaviors. Sometimes the call to grow and change is just too frightening and overwhelming for us.

Another source of our refusal to accept God's forgiveness may be our pride. We have free will; accepting God's forgiveness demands action on our part. Maybe we must make an act of trust in God's forgiveness. Perhaps we will receive a call to obey by living according to God's will. What will we have to give up? What are we clinging to that may be sinful? Am I sorry enough to let God take control of my life? We are called to admit we do not know better than He does, to let go of our assumptions and believe what He tells us.

In Isaiah 1:18, we read, "Though your sins be like scarlet, they may become white as snow; Though they be crimson red, they may become white as wool." What a promise!

As we go through this day, let us pray for those who are hanging on to unhealthy behaviors and refusing the mercy of God, that they may have a change of heart and allow Him to heal them, knowing that He always desires their salvation.

> When we return to him, he welcomes us as children, in his house, because he never gives up waiting for us with love, not even for a moment. And his heart is in celebration for every child who returns.
>
> — Pope Francis, Sunday *Angelus*, Vatican City, September 15, 2013

Were a soul like a decaying corpse so that from a human standpoint, there would be no [hope of] **restoration and everything would already be lost, it is not so with God. The miracle of Divine Mercy restores that soul in full.**

— *Diary*, 1448

An Unrepentant Heart

"Theresa, you need to accept the possibility that your father may never repent of your abortion." I will never forget my spiritual director's words. For years, I had been praying a novena to Our Lady of Czestochowa, the patroness of the *Entering Canaan* post-abortion ministry I have developed with the Sisters of Life, asking for my father's conversion of heart.

Coerced into abortion as a teen by my dad, I had made it a daily practice to ask Our Lady to bring him to the mercy of her Son. I had said that prayer every day for over 20 years. The thought that my dad might never open himself up to the graces made available through Our Lady's loving intercession was something I did not want to accept.

Forgiving my dad was not easy. I wish I could say he thought he was doing what was best for me when he forced me to abort, but in reality, my dad was concerned about the way things looked to others. I have since learned he was involved in other abortions.

The death of my unborn child altered my entire life. My struggles with abandonment and unforgiveness were not easily overcome. Only through my own healing and the grace of God was I able to begin to show my father the mercy and forgiveness that God had shown to me.

At the end of his life, thankfully, my dad did repent. He went to Confession. During our last conversation, I told him to hug my unborn son when he saw him in Heaven. My father's conversion, late in life though it happened, is a reminder that Christ came to call sinners, and that we need to learn the lessons of Advent and be patient and wait, because we never know how God is working. Yes, there are those who will continue to refuse the mercy of God, but it is our job to keep offering it to them, never knowing if, in that last second, they will repent. As St. Faustina writes in her *Diary*, "God's mercy sometimes touches the sinner at the last moment in a wondrous and mysterious way. Outwardly, it seems as if everything were lost, but it is not so. The soul, illumined by a ray of God's powerful final grace, turns to God in the last moment with such a power of love that, in an instant, it receives from God forgiveness of sin and punishment, while outwardly it shows no sign either of repentance or of contrition, because souls [at that stage] no longer react to external things. Oh, how beyond comprehension is God's mercy!" (1698).

> Now under the attacks of the world, which speaks to us of our sins, we see that the ability to repent is a grace, and we see how it is necessary to repent, that is, to recognize what is wrong in our life.
>
> — Pope Benedict XVI, Homily, Vatican, April 15, 2010

I must never judge anyone, but look at others with leniency and at myself with severity. I must refer everything to God and, in my own eyes, recognize myself for what I am: utter misery and nothingness. In suffering, I must be patient and quiet, knowing that everything passes in time.

— *Diary*, 253

Sorrow

Have mercy on me, O God, according to thy
steadfast love; according to thy abundant
mercy blot out my transgressions.

Wash me thoroughly from my iniquity,
and cleanse me from my sin!

For I know my transgressions,
and my sin is ever before me. ...

For thou hast no delight in sacrifice;
were I to give a burnt offering,
thou wouldst not be pleased.

The sacrifice acceptable to God is a broken spirit;
a broken and contrite heart, O God,
thou wilt not despise.

— Ps 51: 1-3, 16-17

Psalm 51 is one of my favorites. It reminds me that I always need to bring to God my sorrow and humility, a knowledge that I am human and will be on a journey to Him for my entire life on earth. I will fall along my way, but the important thing is not to get discouraged. Rather, I need to pick myself up, clean myself off in the Sacraments, and get moving again. I am not speaking about my abortion here. Once sin is forgiven in the Sacrament of Reconciliation, it is forgiven for all time. But I need to bring my sorrow and humility to God over and over again for all of my sins.

I need to remember that all the good I do comes from Him and belongs to Him. My healing is a gift freely given; I am called to show that same compassion to others. After all, who needed mercy more than I did?

When I am judgmental or impatient with others, I need to keep my sin always before me and remember what the Lord has done for me and how compassionate He is. I need to remember that I am called to show the same mercy to others that I have been shown, knowing we are all in need of God's mercy.

Many post-abortive men and women feel judged by both the pro-choice and pro-life sides. It can be very difficult. Today, as a way of sharing God's mercy with others, pray for those who you feel have judged you.

> When someone learns to accuse oneself, one is merciful toward others: "Yes, but who am I to judge if I am capable of doing worse things?"
>
> — Pope Francis, Homily, Domus Sanctae Marthae,
> March 2, 2015

Thank You, Jesus, for the great favor of making known to me the whole abyss of my misery. I know that I am an abyss of nothingness and that, if Your holy grace did not hold me up, I would return to nothingness in a moment. And so, with every beat of my heart, I thank You, my God, for Your great mercy towards me.

— *Diary*, 256

Remember You are Dust!

"Remember that you are dust, and to dust you shall return."

I have always considered these words striking, and to be honest, ones I did not like to hear. Talk about a wakeup call! They are a reminder of my vulnerability and mortality, the fact that this life will one day end and my body placed into the ground to decay.

Each year on Ash Wednesday, these words echo in my head as the priest makes the Sign of the Cross on my forehead. It really could be a downer, if not for the fact that I know that better things — actually, the best things — are yet to come on my demise.

I did not always feel this way. For years, I shunned the Church, terrified, hiding from my mortality and living in despair because I thought my death would mean eternity in hell. I placed all of the focus on me, instead of on Jesus Christ and exactly what Lent and His life mean for us.

Lent is a time for sacrifice and prayer, a time to reflect on the ultimate act of love: Jesus Christ dying on the Cross for our sins. It took no act of ours to get Him to do it. He willingly suffered and died so that we could come to know His great love and mercy for us. Through the pain and suffering He endured on the Cross, I am now also able to see the tremendous love He has for each one of us — a love that frees us from all of our sins, even the sin of abortion!

Do not abandon yourselves to despair. We are the Easter people and hallelujah is our song.

— Pope John Paul II, Apostolic Journey to the Far East and Oceania, *Angelus*, November 30, 1986

Even though a soul may immediately distinguish between false inspiration and those of God, it should nevertheless be careful, because many things are uncertain. God is pleased and rejoices when a soul distrusts Him for His own sake; because it loves Him, it is prudent and itself asks and searches for help to make certain that it is really God who is acting within it. And once a well-instructed confessor has confirmed this, the soul should be at peace and give itself up to God, according to His directions; that is, according to the directions of the confessor.

—Diary, 139

Penance as a Transformation in Healing

I have spoken a lot about our inability to "earn" God's forgiveness by things we may do. The good news is that the price of our forgiveness was paid on the Cross by Jesus Christ, and that costly forgiveness is a gift freely given. That being said, there is a place for penance in healing from abortion, but it is a place of gratitude and a desire to make amends, not a place of desperation or a hopeless struggle to pay the price for forgiveness.

Penance comes in at least two different forms. The penance given to us in the Sacrament of Confession is a necessary component of obtaining the freely-given gift of forgiveness of our sin. This penance aids in our personal conversion. It does not serve to atone for our abortion — the Body and Blood, Soul and Divinity of Jesus alone serves to do that — but to assist us in belonging more fully to Christ.

The other form of penance we may do is out of love and gratitude to Jesus, so that I may unite myself and my sufferings to Him and His Passion.

Last year, Fr. Mariusz Koch, CFR; Fr. Conrad Osterhaut, CFR; and I led a pilgrimage of women and men who have had an abortion. It was an act of reparation and love, responding to our past sins of abortion. One of the most moving moments in this pilgrimage was a prayer service, during which each of us placed a heart with our child's name written on it at the base of a cross atop a mountain. In exchange, we were each given a blessed replica of the cross to bring home with us. We had symbolically made an "exchange with God."

In the end, the pilgrimage was a tremendous gift to us from God, as we prayed together daily and made sacrifices for those still separated from Him because of the sin of abortion.

Acts of reparation and penance are good and necessary for our personal transformation and for the conversion of souls, but we must always be careful to have the direction of a good spiritual advisor to make certain we are not making these acts out of our pride or self-will, but truly are doing His will.

This dying to self for the good of our own souls and the souls of others is necessary in the journey towards healing, which is ongoing, but true penance is very different from thinking we can earn forgiveness.

May we all prayerfully do acts of reparation under the direction of a spiritual advisor out of love for God.

"[W]e Christians, even in recent times," he [Pope Benedict XVI] said, "have often avoided the word 'penance,' which seemed too harsh to us. Now ... we see that being able to do penance is a grace and we see how it is necessary to do penance, that is, to recognize what is mistaken in our life, to open oneself to forgiveness, to prepare oneself for forgiveness, to allow oneself to be transformed. The pain of penance, that is to say of purification and of transformation, this pain is grace, because it is renewal, and it is the work of Divine Mercy."

— Pope Benedict XVI, Homily, Private Vatican Mass,
April 15, 2010

My daughter, do whatever is within your power to spread devotion to My mercy. I will make up for what you lack. Tell aching mankind to snuggle close to My merciful Heart, and I will fill it with peace.

Tell [all people]**, My daughter, that I am Love and Mercy itself. When a soul approaches Me with trust, I fill it with such an abundance of graces that it cannot contain them within itself, but radiates them to other souls.**

— *Diary*, 1074

Allowing People to Help You

If you are like I was, you find it very hard to ask for or accept help from anyone after your abortion. I had major trust issues and did not want to be vulnerable. The vulnerability I felt at the time of my abortion, both before and after, was enough to last a lifetime.

I would shy away from people offering help, convincing myself I was not worthy to receive any. After all, I did not want to "bother" anyone; I was going to do it all myself. Who needs people when they fail you, anyway?

It took me a long time to admit that my pride was stopping me from requesting or accepting help. I was afraid of rejection, of being let down again, of letting people see my struggles. Now, I am not talking about withholding my struggles from people who were not capable of being there, but rather of refusing to open up to good people who truly wanted to help.

It was so hard for me to allow anyone to help me. At first, I only did it out of desperation. Perhaps God brought me to that place of desperation so I would see how much I needed to meet Him through other people.

I viewed needing help as a weakness, but as I came to know Him, I also came to learn that we need to allow people to help us just as much as we need to help other people. "Love one another as I have loved you" (Jn 15:12), and He loved us enough to allow us to help Him in His humanity.

I love the Sixth Station of the Cross, when Veronica wipes the face of Jesus. He — God Himself — does not push her away and say, "I am God; I do not need your help." Instead, He humbles Himself and allows her this *gift* of wiping His face. In return for her kindness, He leaves her the image of His face imprinted on the cloth.

When we feel like we do not want to ask for help or allow others to help us, whether we are struggling with our abortion, healing, or any other issue, let us remember Jesus and His humble willingness to allow Veronica to wipe His face. Let us reach out for the help we need.

> Mercy is love that suffers the evil of another to affirm his dignity so that he does not have to suffer alone.
>
> — Pope John Paul II, World Youth Day in Toronto, Canada, July 27, 2002

My daughter, I want to teach you about spiritual warfare. Never trust in yourself, but abandon yourself totally to my will. In desolation, darkness and various doubts, have recourse to Me and to your spiritual director. [...] Do not bargain with any temptation; lock yourself immediately in My Heart [...]. Put your self-love in the last place, so that it does not taint your deeds. [...] Shun murmurers like a plague. Let all act as they like; you are to act as I want you to.

— *Diary,* 1760

Temptation

In the Gospel, we read how Jesus remained in the desert for 40 days and was tempted by Satan.

We are often tempted in the course of the healing process, even if we have gone to the Sacrament of Reconciliation. Those temptations can include temptations to despair, to old behaviors, to unforgiveness toward others or ourselves, or even the belief that God has not forgiven us — the list goes on and on.

Temptations are not in themselves sins. It is what we do in response to temptation that can be sinful. It is important to nip them in the bud so that they do not grow into actions. Jesus prayed to God and fasted during His time of temptation. He used those temptations as an occasion to pray to His Father and grow stronger in His resolve. He knew that Satan is a liar and God is love and mercy.

The next time you are tempted to despair during your healing process, feel like you are going nowhere, and want to give up, use the occasion as an opportunity to proclaim your trust in God instead, in spite of what you are feeling.

Pray! Offer up this trial for someone in need of God's grace. Most importantly, reach out for help by picking up the phone and speaking to someone who can walk with you through it.

The devil wants to isolate us so he can fill our heads with his lies. Like Jesus, always remember: God always loves you and is there with you, even when you cannot feel His presence.

> The image of the wilderness is a very eloquent metaphor of the human condition. The book of Exodus narrates the experience of the people of Israel that, after having come out of Egypt, wandered in the Sinai desert during 40 years, before reaching the Promised Land.
>
> During this long journey, the Jews experienced all the force and insistence of the tempter that led them to lose confidence in the Lord and to turn back; but, at the same time, thanks to the mediation of Moses, they learned to listen to the voice of the Lord, who was calling them to become his holy people.
>
> — Pope Benedict XVI, *Angelus*, St. Peter's Square, March 5, 2006

Be at peace, My daughter, it is precisely through such misery that I want to show the power of My mercy.

— *Diary*, 133

Where Mercy Meets Faithfulness

It is the point of healing, the place where ultimate pain joins with ultimate love in an act of complete trust and surrender. There, we climb on the Cross with Christ to join mercy with faithfulness.

I can remember the struggle to be faithful, searching in the dark to find God, holding on to His Word because I had tried everything else and longed to be healed. I remember having to keep moving in spite of the pain, the darkness, the fear, because there was nothing to lose. There could be no greater hell than the one I had made for myself.

I begged and pleaded with God, reminding Him of His promises, asking Him to be faithful to them in spite of my failures. I worked at chipping the remains of the old me away, fighting myself so I could reach complete surrender.

There were many times when I needed encouragement to continue in spite of my temptations and bouts with despair, pushing through the times when I felt I could not go on. God provided the people necessary to give me the push that I needed, the words I had to hear, the strength to hang on.

I continually pleaded for the saints' intercession and especially entrusted myself to Mary and Joseph.

Finally, one day, alone with Jesus (because He is the only one who can heal), I trusted enough to climb onto the Cross, to be one with the pain and the love that exists there, and to allow that love to fill my deep wounds.

There, His mercy met my faith, and I finally felt healed of my abortion. I suddenly understood so much of Scripture. So much of it was then fulfilled in me, such a gift given. I felt like Mary Magdalene at the foot of the Cross. Immense love had taken on immense sin and had washed away its stains.

To be sure, the process of healing from abortion is painful and delicate, but with the right help and trust in God, even if that process is not "felt," it is possible. Jesus in His mercy longs to heal us. We need to persevere in our faithfulness and light the way for others.

> ... And in the desert people of faith are needed who, with their own lives, point out the way to the Promised Land and keep hope alive.

> — Pope Benedict XVI, Homily,
> Opening of the Year of Faith, October 11, 2012

Spring

Jesus: **O soul steeped in darkness, do not despair. All is not yet lost. Come and confide in your God, who is love and mercy.**

[...]

In the soul arises this reply: "For me there is no mercy," and it falls into greater darkness, a despair which is a foretaste of hell and makes it unable to draw near to God.

Jesus calls to the soul a third time, but the soul remains deaf and blind, hardened and despairing. Then the mercy of God begins to exert itself, and without any co-operation from the soul, God grants it final grace. If this too is spurned, God will leave the soul in this self-chosen disposition for eternity. This grace emerges from the merciful Heart of Jesus and gives the soul a special light by means of which the soul begins to understand God's effort; but conversion depends on its own will. The soul knows that this, for her, is final grace and, should it show even a flicker of good will, the mercy of God will accomplish the rest.

— *Diary*, 1486

The Judas in Us

We all know who Judas Iscariot was. For 30 pieces of silver, he betrayed his friend Jesus Christ. For three years he had followed this Man, yet in spite of being His apostle, he did not truly know Him. We cannot know for sure what prompted this betrayal. We all tend to think that if we were in such a situation, we would never do such a thing. How could he? This was the Savior, the Messiah. Judas was in the presence of God. It all seems so clear to us. Whatever Judas' motive for betrayal — whether it was greed, power, or fear — we can safely assume its roots were in self-love.

After the arrest of Jesus, Judas realized what he had done. We are told he repented and brought the 30 pieces of silver back to the chief priests, saying, "I have sinned in betraying innocent blood" (Mt 27:4), but the chief priests and elders said, "What is that to us? See to it thyself" (Mt 27:5). At that, Judas flung the silver pieces into the temple, withdrew, "and went away and hanged himself with a halter" (Mt 27:5).

What was Judas' biggest sin? Most of us would say the betrayal of Jesus. But that is not it. Judas' greatest sin was his despair. Even after living with Jesus for three years, hearing Him preach, and witnessing his miracles, Judas still didn't believe that the unlimited love and mercy of God was bigger than any sin he had committed. Had he only gone to Jesus in his sorrow and repentance, he would have been forgiven. Judas believed in and hated himself more than he believed in Jesus. He thought that he had committed the unforgivable sin. Judas put himself in the place of God, believing himself to be the only person he could ultimately trust. He doubted Jesus' love for him.

All too often, we who are post-abortive believe, like Judas, that we have committed the unforgivable sin. It is hard for us to imagine God taking us in His arms and saying, "Your sins are forgiven you." Often, even if we have gone to the Sacrament of Reconciliation, we still feel unforgiven. How can forgiveness be possible when we are responsible for the death of our very own child? What sin could be worse?

The key to coming to feel this unfathomable forgiveness and mercy is knowing Jesus Christ who is living in our midst, understanding that His ways are not our ways and that His mercy and love are truly bigger than any sin we are capable of committing. It is a firm belief in His promises. It is forgiving ourselves because to do less would be an insult to God. It is loving Him more than ourselves because He is God and "worthy of all our love." If He can really forgive us, who are we to deny ourselves that forgiveness?

> Who can say that he is free from sin and does not need God's mercy? As people of this restless time of ours, wavering between the emptiness of self-exaltation and the humiliation of despair, we have a greater need than ever for a regenerating experience of mercy.
>
> — Pope John Paul II, Divine Mercy Sunday,
> April 10, 1994

I accept joy or suffering, praise or humiliation with the same disposition. I remember that one and the other are passing. What does it matter to me what people say about me? I have long ago given up everything that concerns my person. My name is host — or sacrifice, not in words but in deeds, in the emptying of myself and in becoming like You on the Cross, O Good Jesus, my Master!

— *Diary*, 485

How Can You Mend a Broken Heart?

As we enter the Triduum, we accompany Jesus on His journey to the Cross and our salvation. It is a deep suffering, but at the same time, a comfort to know that He shared so much of what we have suffered in life, though in a much deeper way because He was without sin. He *willingly* took on this suffering to pay the price for our sins.

For three years, the apostles had been with Jesus. They had witnessed many miracles, listened for hours to His teachings, and shared life intimately with Him. Yet we see the betrayal of Judas, the denial of Peter, and the scattering of all the rest of the apostles, with the exception of John who returned after fleeing.

I cannot help but think of how Jesus' Heart must have broken as His closest friends betrayed, denied, and abandoned Him. I am sure He had hoped to see the love He had shown them manifested. Yet He knew they were weak, even imploring them in the Garden of Gethsemane, "Watch and pray that you may not undergo the test" (Mt 26:41).

They were fallen human beings, with human weaknesses. Their fear, pride, anxiety, etc., would cause them to act as if they had not known Him at all, as if they could do good of their own strength. In their fall is the story of man and the heartbreak of Jesus.

We can relate on some level. At one time or another in life, we will all suffer from a broken heart. Those human beings whom we love and trust have failed us in some way. Perhaps that failure was in the context of our abortion; maybe someone we thought loved us coerced us into getting an abortion. Maybe close friends or family members seemed to have no regard for our feelings, or used us for their own ends. In the wake of such failures, we are left with a broken heart because we truly believed in their love and cannot understand how they could have hurt us so deeply.

But we are all human, all fallen, all sinners in need of God's grace and mercy.

As we contemplate the agony of Jesus, let us remember there is a way to mend a broken heart. It may take time, and we may need to choose to accept being healed from deep hurt over and over again, but Christ gives us a way. The way is **Him**. By keeping our eyes on Christ, we can make the decision to heal, no matter how painful the process.

By knowing in our broken hearts that He understands our pain; by trusting Him, and then trusting Him some more, and then even more, even when we feel no trust; and then deciding to trust in Him and His love for us again, knowing that He is always there, He can heal our deep pain by means of His own.

God's promises are true. His mercy is real. Yes, we have things we must do in order to heal. We may need to change behaviors and learn to deal with the psychological consequences of abortion or any other wound we may have in order to heal. As we do all that, we also need to hand over our broken hearts to God, who never fails to mend them through His Passion, Death, and Resurrection.

> I see the church as a field hospital after battle. It is useless to ask a seriously injured person if he has high cholesterol and about the level of his blood sugars. You have to heal his wounds. Then we can talk about everything else.
>
> — Pope Francis, interview, Rome, August 2013.
> The interview was conducted in person
> by Antonio Spadaro, SJ, editor in chief of
> *La Civiltà Cattolica*, the Italian Jesuit journal.

Amid the greatest torments, I fix the gaze of my soul upon Jesus Crucified; I do not expect help from people, but place my trust in God. In His unfathomable mercy lies all my hope.

— *Diary*, 681

The Agony in the Garden

Post-abortive people know agony, the agony of realizing they participated in the death of their child through abortion. Often, it is something they live with every day of their lives.

Many times, those struggling to heal are not able to understand that having faith and accepting healing often have nothing to do with what we are feeling. Some people think that if you feel sad or are struggling, you do not have faith or may be ungrateful, but the agony of Jesus in the Garden of Gethsemane shows us differently. We are fully human, as Jesus was, and what we feel does not define our faith.

There is no doubt that our Lord had complete, trustful surrender to the will of His Heavenly Father, yet Jesus cried out in the Garden. He suffered. He was in pain. He felt fear. He even felt abandoned by God. But in spite of those feelings, He fulfilled the will of His Father in the midst of His pain and suffering.

We, too, may cry out when we are being assailed by the memories and wounds from our abortion, when the tempters whisper terrible things in our ears, or, for that matter, when we confront other struggles in life. It does not mean we do not trust in God or even that we are ungrateful. God wants us to cry out to Him in all our needs! It just means we are human, and humans suffer in life. In fact, it is an opportunity for us to show God how much we do trust in Him.

What we do with that suffering is key. Do we persevere, as Jesus did, in doing God's will? Do we pray and reach out to those who can help us, or do we sit in isolation? And if we are not the ones who are suffering, do we help others to carry their crosses instead of merely telling them they should not feel that way, and thus learn to grow in love?

The proof of our faith is not in *feelings*. Feeling good is not something we may choose to do; it is a gift. Faith is in *knowing and believing* in the promises of Christ, in *knowing and believing* He came down to earth to pay the ransom for our sins (yes, including our sin of abortion as well as all our other sins, no matter what they are). Our faith should rest in knowing and believing He loves us, no matter how we feel, and that we love Him, no matter how we feel.

Yes, Jesus suffered His agony in the Garden, an agony that came from taking on the weight of the sins of the world, and yet He continued to trust. May we always continue to trust, no matter what we feel, knowing His love and mercy for us endure forever (see Ps 136).

Jesus says: "Father, for you all things are possible; remove this cup from me; yet not what I want, but what you want" (Mk 14:36). The natural will of the man Jesus recoils in fear before the enormity of the matter. He asks to be spared. Yet as the Son, he places this human will into the Father's will: not I, but you. In this way he transformed the stance of Adam, the primordial human sin, and thus heals humanity.

> — Pope Benedict XVI, Homily,
> Mass of the Last Supper, April 5, 2012

Jesus: **Poor soul, I see that you suffer much and that you do not have even the strength to converse with me. So I will speak to you. Even though your sufferings were very great, do not lose heart or give in to despondency. But tell Me, my child, who has dared to wound your heart? Tell me about everything, be sincere in dealing with Me, reveal all the wounds of your heart. I will heal them, and your suffering will become a source of your sanctification.**

— *Diary*, 1487

Brokenhearted

It is hard when we struggle to forgive and let go of deep hurt. It is only through God's grace that we are able to do this when people whom we love hurt us deeply, people we truly trusted and thought loved us. Yet we need to *choose* to let go of the pain and the hurt, to follow Christ.

It is at times like this that we truly know what it means to be brokenhearted, and times like this when we learn how close Jesus is to us. When we trust people enough to share with them that which is most dear to us and our treasure is not treated with the respect and dignity it deserves, but rather is used for some agenda, it is very painful. When the cross of betrayal keeps on giving, it is so hard to continue to choose to forgive — but forgive we must.

When this happens, we truly share in the suffering of Christ. We must continue to pray for the grace not to be resentful, bitter, or angry, but rather to make the choice to forgive, even to forgive every day, if we have to. It is hard to forgive when you are in deep pain, but it is a choice that we need to continue to make because of our love for God and because, in the end, that is what is really important: sharing the mercy we have received. That is the way to true healing, freedom, and peace.

From the Cross, we hear Jesus ask His Father to forgive those who have crucified Him. We have heard it a million times, but when we are deeply suffering, Christ's words take on new meaning. Christ forgave from the Cross!

He did not forgive when He was feeling better, or when things settled down and He had risen from the grave. He forgave from that very place of excruciating pain. He chose to forgive even in the midst of being betrayed, enduring physical and mental pain, even in the agony of His Crucifixion! He chose to conquer sin with His love and forgiveness and mercy. By His grace, may we do the same.

> In biblical language, heart indicates a person's center, seat of his feelings and intentions. In the Heart of the Redeemer, we adore God's love of humanity, His will of universal salvation, His infinite mercy. Worship of the Sacred Heart of Christ means, therefore, worship of that Heart which, after having loved us to the end, was pierced by the spear, and from the cross on high, shed blood and water, inexhaustible source of new life.
>
> — Pope Benedict XVI, *Angelus*, 5 June 2005

My daughter, try your best to make the Stations of the Cross in this hour [3 p.m., the Hour of Great Mercy], provided that your duties permit it; and if you are not able to make the Stations of the Cross, then at least step into the chapel for a moment and adore, in the Blessed Sacrament, My Heart, which is full of mercy; and should you be unable to step into the chapel, immerse yourself in prayer there where you happen to be, if only for a very brief instant.

— *Diary*, 1572

In the Cross is Salvation

I love the cross. I hate the cross. The spiritual side of my human nature embraces it; my worldly side wants to throw it as far away from me as I can. The truth is, the cross is unavoidable — we all get to bear a cross whether we want to or not.

In the midst of deep suffering, it is hard to remember that this is what brings us salvation (see Mt 16:24; Lk 9:23). We are tossed around, feeling like we are barely clinging to sanity. We often feel we are losing ourselves. We find ourselves trying to force our will to choose to continue to trust in God in spite of how we feel. We are suddenly living our faith, a faith of paradoxes where our answers are found in the places we humanly do not want to go. It is painful, often threatening, and a fearful place to be, but we are told by Jesus and St. John Paul II, "Be not afraid."

It is in this place, at this cross, that we meet the merciful love of the crucified Christ.

> The Cross is the most profound bowing down of the Divinity towards man ... the Cross is like a touch of eternal love on the most painful wounds of humanity's earthly existence.
>
> — Pope John Paul II, quoted in Pope Benedict XVI, Encounter with the sick, Krakow, Lagiewniki, May 26, 2006

I desire trust from My creatures. Encourage souls to place great trust in My fathomless mercy. Let the weak, sinful soul have no fear to approach Me, for even if it had more sins than there are grains of sand in the world, all would be drowned in the unmeasurable depths of My mercy.

— *Diary*, 1059

Choosing Divine Mercy

There is a beautiful Eucharistic Prayer in the Catholic Church that says this: "God of love and mercy, You are always ready to forgive, we are sinners and You invite us to trust in Your mercy." He does not force us; He invites us. He tells us His mercy is there for us, but it is up to us if we accept His invitation.

Mary had been to Confession multiple times before she came to our *Entering Canaan* post-abortion ministry retreat. She often shared, "I have confessed my abortion so many times, but I just do not feel forgiven." Because of various circumstances in her life, Mary had not been able to accept the mercy of God.

It is not unusual for someone who has been involved in an abortion to voice those feelings in spite of having gone to the Sacrament of Reconciliation. They do not feel the forgiveness, the "mercy" of God. In fact, more often than not, an abortion will be confessed over and over again. As human beings, so much of what we believe is based on our feelings or memories of past experiences, which very often may not reflect truth. *Being* forgiven and *feeling* forgiven are two very different things.

One part of the problem is being unable to forgive yourself. Another, I believe, is an inability to accept that walking into a confessional and telling a priest about your abortion, and then receiving a penance of three or 3,000 Hail Marys will somehow equate to forgiveness for participating in the death of your own child. It just seems way too easy — and it is!

We can never make up for our abortions, and three or 3,000 Hail Marys is not going to do it. Neither is speaking out, working in ministry, or praying in front of an abortion clinic (which does not mean that these works of mercy should not be done). There is only one thing that atones for the sin of abortion (or, for that matter, any sin), and that is the Passion, Death, Resurrection, and Ascension of Jesus Christ. This is His gift of mercy, freely given to us.

Mary Ellen puts it this way: "At first, 'mercy' was just a word, an idea, which in my mind vaguely was synonymous with compassion and forgiveness. I heard it in the prayers and blessings at the Gatherings [*Entering Canaan* post-abortion groups] I attended. I heard it constantly. Every piece of writing from the *Entering Canaan* post-abortion ministry echoed the word 'mercy.' Over the years without my knowing it, the word 'mercy' became for me a kind of mantra, something to hold on to in the dark. It began to work on me without my knowing it."

That is a great way to think of God's mercy: "something to hold on to in the dark," even when we are devoid of feelings, *knowing* God is mercy while in the dark! We must make a choice to believe in this mercy.

We should not believe that somehow, our feelings are a gauge of whether we have been forgiven — they aren't. Kathy had gone on a weekend retreat and left feeling totally healed and forgiven. She was experiencing a spiritual high. However, as the days went on and the old familiar tapes of despair begin to play in her head again, the "stinking thinking of abortion" once again told her she was not forgiven or healed. "He healed everyone else on that weekend, but not me," she said. "My sin must be worse; He loves and forgave other retreatants, but not me." Kathy was suffering from the same reaction to a lack of feelings as Mary. They were basing their belief in God's forgiveness on how they felt, instead of on the truth. If you go make a valid Confession and receive absolution, you are forgiven, no matter what sin you confess or the circumstances around it!

Healing from abortion is a multifaceted process. In addition to going to Confession and growing in your relationship with God, a post-abortive person needs to develop his or her understanding of the dynamics of abortion and the reasons it happened. Identifying personal abortion connectors (people, places, or things that bring back the trauma of abortion) is also key in the healing process, as well as delving into other areas of life that became manifest before or after the abortion. Dealing with abuse, addiction, disorders, etc., is instrumental in healing from your abortion.

As a person moves through this process, it may often feel as though they are moving backwards. Thus, making the choice to trust in the mercy of God no matter what is crucial. As they grow in their relationship with Him, they are able to more freely look honestly at their lives, no matter what they have done, because they know they are unconditionally loved. Having the support of others through ministry, professional counseling, and/or spiritual direction is also crucial.

As Mary Ellen says so well, "I am learning mercy, because it is a process and a journey into the kind of deep love and forgiveness of myself — and others — that I can only begin to grasp. From my beginning, almost neutral experience with 'mercy' as a simple word, it has evolved in my life experience as a tangible and effective tool, an action verb that I have learned can more quickly than I ever imagined bring a swift conclusion to the obsessive dark voice that would grind my spirit with self-recrimination and unbelief. Be gone, Satan!"

"Mercy is a way of life, and it is life-changing. Now whenever darkness calls, I choose mercy and life."

Do you choose mercy?

> I am one who is looked upon by the Lord. I always felt my motto, *Miserando atque Eligendo* [By Having Mercy and by Choosing Him], was very true for me.
>
> — Pope Francis, Nicole Winfield, "Pope's likes, dislike, daily routine and favorite foods," AP, Sept. 19, 2015

[Let] **the greatest sinners place their trust in My mercy. They have the right before others to trust in the abyss of My mercy. My daughter, write about My mercy towards tormented souls. Souls that make an appeal to My mercy delight Me. To such souls I grant even more graces than they ask. I cannot punish even the greatest sinner if he makes an appeal to My compassion, but on the contrary, I justify him in My unfathomable and inscrutable mercy.**

— *Diary*, 1146

Trusting in God's Mercy

Anyone who knows me also knows that I end every witness talk with these words of Jesus from St. Faustina's *Diary* (above).

I can still remember the first time I read those words, "the greatest sinner!" That was me! He was speaking to me! Who could possibly be a worse sinner than I, who had aborted a baby in my fourth month of pregnancy?

I remember contemplating the "abyss" of God's mercy, limitless, infinite, never-ending, a great enough supply to fill the deep recesses of the wounds of abortion. Not only was I being told it was there, but I was being told I had "the right before others to trust!" What could possibly give me, such a great sinner, this right, and how did I possibly deserve it?

As good as it all sounded, I could see no way it could possibly be true, considering who I was and what I had done.

I continued to be hung up on the belief that I did not deserve His mercy or forgiveness. Surely, this was meant for everyone but me!

But then something happened. As I traveled down my road of healing, learning the dynamics of life post-abortion, and growing in my faith relationship with Jesus, I came to take the focus off of myself and place it on Him, instead. I came to see that of course I did not deserve His Mercy: That was the point. I was a sinner who had committed a grave sin, but my healing and His mercy were not about me.

Although I was called to look at my abortion — not to blame myself or others, but to understand what had happened — I was also called to look at the life of Jesus. It was there in Him that I began to understand how healing was possible.

> We, who were slaves of sin — He has made us all free … He has healed us at the very core of our existence.
>
> — Pope Francis, Homily, Domus Sanctae Marthae,
> April 7, 2013

Therefore, let every soul trust in the Passion of the Lord, and place its hope in His mercy. God will not deny His mercy to anyone.

— *Diary*, 72

A Sign of Hope

The initial day of the *Entering Canaan* post-abortion ministry's retreat is called "A Day of Prayer & Healing," and is the first in a series of events on the road towards healing. Our goal for this one day is to bring those who come to us — shattered, shame-filled, sorrowful, and often despairing from a past abortion — to the knowledge that there *is* hope of healing. In fact, it is God's desire that they be healed and have joy in their lives again. If the people who participate in this first day leave with that hope in their hearts, the day was successful.

There are many dynamics in post-abortion healing. Each person is unique, and we strive to honor his or her dignity by respecting that uniqueness. Some may reach healing quickly, while others have suffered many wounds and may take longer to heal. We trust in God's goodness and His love for each person, and know that He is working in their lives and wants to heal each one to their core.

Many of the people who come to us have a common feeling of being judged by others. This judgment often confirms for them how they already feel — as though they cannot be forgiven. It leaves them with no hope of healing and a fear of coming forward because they do not believe mercy is available to them. Many have kept their abortions hidden, living with the fear of being found out.

The Gospels call us all to be careful of judging others, whether we are tempted to judge those who have had abortions or those who may condemn post-abortive people. Jesus calls us to see we are all in need of His mercy, and so this same mercy should be shown to others.

May all of us reflect the mercy of Christ in the world, and when we feel judged or condemned, may we offer a prayer for the person doing the judging instead of getting angry. May we each be a sign of Christ's *hope* in the world, knowing that He is showing us the same mercy we are called to show others.

> To protect creation, to protect every man and every woman, to look upon them with tenderness and love, is to open up a horizon of hope; it is to let a shaft of light break through the heavy clouds; it is to bring the warmth of hope!
>
> — Pope Francis, Homily, St. Peter's Square, Tuesday, 19 March 2013, Solemnity of St. Joseph

At that moment, I realized I was entering into communion with the incomprehensible Majesty. I felt that God was waiting for my word, for my consent. Then my spirit immersed itself in the Lord, and I said, "Do with me as You please. I subject myself to Your will. As of today, Your holy will shall be my nourishment, and I will be faithful to Your commands with the help of Your grace. Do with me as You please. I beg You, O Lord, be with me at every moment of my life."

— *Diary*, 136

Jesus Passes Our Way

I will never forget that moment, which dwells in my heart as a living memory; a meeting of hearts that forever is implanted on my soul; an instant of knowing His touch that no one can take away from me, an encounter with Mercy Himself that would change me forever.

Throughout my healing process, I struggled with depression. I would beg Jesus for healing. I felt bad that I had not experienced a full healing, and my confessor's eyes showed his own sadness over my continued struggle. I understand now that the fullness of healing must come in God's own time, not ours.

One night I felt depressed and suicidal again, but despite these feelings, I also somehow had a deep trust in God. I didn't want the children to see me crying, so after putting them to bed, I closed myself in the bathroom, crouched on the floor, and repeated over and over, "Jesus, I trust in You."

I don't know how many hours I prayed like that, but deep into the night, I had an experience that changed my life. I experienced being on the Cross with Christ. But instead of encountering suffering, I felt love so intense that it was capable of taking away my pain. In that moment, I knew that my healing was complete.

I have never since sensed the despair of abortion, but only the profound love and forgiveness Christ has given me. I've watched my life transform miraculously as I have been privileged to help countless women and men who are suffering abortion's aftermath. Christ's love transformed not only my life, but also the lives of those I love.

That one moment has been the basis of all the work I have done in developing both *Entering Canaan* and Lumina. That moment has given me unshakable confidence because I have confidence in Him, not in anything I may or may not do. That moment bestowed on me the ability to let go and a freedom from myself that enables me to continue to follow Him, no matter how difficult it may be. It gave me a joy of heart that envelops me in His mercy, no matter what I may be feeling. This healing, this communion with God, is in the present moment, because He is living and loves me right here, right now!

It can be difficult to internalize these truths as we seek healing from abortion. Often it is through others that we embark upon the journey, allowing them to guide us down the path to Him. It can be painful and scary, but the assurances of those who have gone before can give us the encouragement to continue, no matter how painful it may be to work through our experiences.

Seek that moment. It is there for you already, waiting to embrace you fully.

> Returning to Galilee means treasuring in my heart the living memory of that call, when Jesus passed my way, gazed at me with mercy, and asked me to follow him … It means reviving the memory of that moment when his eyes met mine, the moment when he made me realize that he loved me.
>
> — Pope Francis, Easter Vigil 2014, Vatican Radio

During the Holy Hour, the Lord allowed me to taste His Passion. I shared in the bitterness of the suffering that filled His soul to overflowing. Jesus gave me to understand how a soul should be faithful to prayer despite torments, dryness, and temptations; because oftentimes the realization of God's great plans depends mainly on such prayer. If we do not persevere in such prayer, we frustrate what the Lord wanted to do through us or within us.

— *Diary*, 872

Perseverance

Blessed is the man ... [whose] delight is in the law of the Lord ... .
He is like a tree planted by streams of water, that yields its fruit in its season.

— Ps 1:3

I am not going to lie: It is not always easy doing post-abortive work. People are more drawn to activism or caring for the unborn, so support for post-abortive people is not always there. I get it. Those of us who are post-abortive are suffering because of our own sin, although some people may be more culpable than others. The unborn are innocents.

But Christ came to call sinners. He came to call you and me. The desire of His heart was to reconcile those far from Him back to His heart. It was not easy for Him, either. He, too, had to persevere in the face of many obstacles as He was "yielding a harvest" for His Father.

I try to embrace this work of helping to bring souls to Christ, and I thank God for the gift of perseverance. I have been so very blessed to see countless souls return to Christ through this work.

While God's mercy is always present in the Church and the world, we especially call out to the depths of His mercy in this time of remembering and reliving the Paschal Mysteries. The commemoration of the Death, Resurrection, and Ascension of Christ gives us hope in the world to come, where we will be united with Him and our children whom we have lost to abortion.

As we approach the Feast of Divine Mercy, may we always remember that our sin is like a drop of water compared to the infinite depths of the ocean of the Divine Mercy of God.

> And the Lord invites us to this: to be rejuvenated Easter people on a journey of love, patience, enduring our tribulations and also — I would say — putting up with one another. We must also do this with charity and love, because if I have to put up with you, I'm sure you will put up with me; and in this way, we will move forward on our journey on the path of Jesus.
>
> — Pope Francis, Homily, May 7, 2013, Vatican Radio

O Mary, my Mother and my Lady, I offer You my soul, my body, my life and my death, and all that will follow it. I place everything in Your hands. O my Mother, cover my soul with Your virginal mantle and grant me the grace of purity of heart, soul and body. Defend me with Your power against all enemies, and especially against those who hide their malice behind the mask of virtue. O lovely lily! You are for me a mirror, O my Mother!

— Diary, 79

Happy Mother's Day

Now, if you are post-abortive, that title probably made you cringe. The day is approaching and most likely, you have already been thinking about it for weeks. The cards are out and the Mother's Day gifts are on the store shelves. There is no escaping it.

For me, this day used to be torture. I can remember one Mother's Day in particular where I spent the day walking around with my two young sons in a stroller. I was crying, trying to stay away from all that would remind me of my child that was not there.

Years later at church, Mother's Day really got to me: "All mothers stand up for a blessing." I remember being mortified. How could I receive a blessing after what I had done? I didn't think I deserved one, and yet if I didn't stand up, they might figure out that I had aborted a baby. Someone I know who is post-abortive and has no living children said to me, "I remember feeling badly about having to sit down." No matter what the circumstances, there is no denying the pain.

Of course, no one who knows about the abortion mentions it. You are left to think you are the only one who remembers. As on many other days, you try to go on with a semblance of normalcy, but inside, your heart is breaking. That is why, years later, at the ministry I co-developed with the Sisters of Life, I decided to meet Mother's Day head on. For our monthly "Gathering" (our post-abortion group meeting), I decided to buy each woman a white rose with a tag attached that said, "Happy Mother's Day, Mom … I miss you. See you in heaven."

The sisters were understandably nervous. Was I sure this was OK? Wouldn't we be bringing back the pain? "No," I assured them. "The pain is already there; we are only acknowledging it and giving them permission to express it."

One by one, the women entered and received their rose. Not one woman was sorry to get it. In fact, it was beautiful. Amidst tears, prayers, and yes, even smiles, each expressed how meaningful it was to them. Their children were real, and so was their motherhood.

Through faith in His love and mercy, we are able with confidence to reclaim our children and become spiritually the mothers we failed to be physically.

We may not be able to hold the physical bodies of our children on earth, but we hold spiritual and emotional ties to them deep in our hearts. By acknowledging our motherhood, we acknowledge our love for our children, consciously making them part of our family, separated by space and time, but joined with us forever by grace and love.

May we entrust ourselves into the hands of Mary, our Mother of Mercy! Happy Mother's Day!

> Mothers always know how to give witness — even in the worst of times — to tenderness, dedication and moral strength.
>
> — Pope Francis, General Audience, January 7, 2015

Oh, if souls would only be willing to listen, at least a little, to the voice of conscience and the voice — that is, the inspirations — of the Holy Spirit! I say "at least a little" because once we open ourselves to the influence of the Holy Spirit, He Himself will fulfill what is lacking in us.

— *Diary*, 359

The Holy Spirit, the Spirit of Truth

The wound in your heart may not yet have healed. Certainly what happened was and remains terribly wrong. But do not give in to discouragement and do not lose hope. Try rather to understand what happened and face it honestly ...

— St. John Paul II, *Evangelium Vitae* (*The Gospel of Life*), 99

As we approach the Feast of Pentecost, we are reminded of the transforming power of the Holy Spirit on the apostles. In an instant, men who had been hiding in the Upper Room, filled with fear and shame, became courageous disciples, proclaiming the Gospel throughout the region. The gifts of the Holy Spirit (wisdom, understanding, counsel, fortitude, knowledge, piety, and fear of the Lord) allowed them to step outside of themselves. The Holy Spirit made the life of Christ live in them, enabling them to see and live in truth, trusting that Jesus' Spirit would guide them.

In his encyclical *The Gospel of Life*, St. John Paul II calls those of us who are post-abortive to live in truth, as well, saying, "Try to understand what happened and face it honestly." But this is impossible if we do not know the love of Jesus Christ and the gifts of the Holy Spirit. Abortion is just too horrific to look at without the light of His love. Like the apostles before the coming of the Holy Spirit, we, too, are fearful, and so we hide in the self-made "upper rooms" of our abortions, full of shame and afraid to stand in the truth. It is only through the life of Christ and His Spirit that we receive the courage and understanding we need to work through our healing process and proclaim the truth of abortion.

As we grow in our faith and travel along the path to healing, we begin to step out in trust. We learn that God does not let us down, as perhaps many people, including ourselves, did when we chose abortion. We come to realize He is Truth and Mercy Itself, and His peace begins to dwell in us. Each gift of the Holy Spirit, the Spirit of Truth, helps us to face our sinfulness in the light of the love of God and to grow, not only in healing, but also in our relationships with Him.

It is not always easy. The ploys of the devil still attempt to create doubt in our minds about God's mercy and forgiveness, but if you continue to trust in spite of what you feel, you will soon come to find the truth never lets you down, and the Truth, who is Jesus Christ Himself, will set you free. So "do not give in to discouragement and do not lose hope" (*The Gospel of Life*). The hope of Christ who frees us from our sins (even our sin of abortion) is there for each one of us through the gifts of His Holy Spirit.

The Spirit is himself the "gift of God, the presence of God's love in the Church and in our hearts."

— Pope Francis, St. Peter's Square, General Audience, Sept, 4, 2014, Vatican Radio

In the Blessed Sacrament, You left us Your mercy;
Your love deigned to arrange it so,
That, going through life, suffering and toil,
I might never doubt of Your goodness and mercy.

— *Diary*, 1748

Does a Mother Forget Her Baby?

I have often read articles on the healing of post-abortive women. It is no surprise that most proclaim there will be suffering that you will carry for the rest of your life. Healing is a long process, and often it is years before a woman moves past the pain. But the truth is, healing *is* possible and she can move past the pain!

It has been years since I last felt the despair and pain I once felt so often from my abortion. Does that mean I am not sorry or that I have forgotten? Of course not, and I would never want to forget; but remembering — even remembering with regret — does not mean that you cannot have joy in your life again.

Most importantly, I would never want to forget. That unborn child was my son Joshua. Far from forgetting, I desire him to be part of my daily life.

It is true I cannot hold him, physically see him, or watch him move through this life, but I can still reclaim him as my child on the spiritual level. I can make him part of my daily life through prayer, trusting that, through God's mercy, he is alive in the same Jesus Christ who gives me life. I can meet my unborn child every day in the Eucharist as I receive Jesus, who, through His presence, unites us to Heaven.

Does a mother forget her child? Thank God, never!

> I would now like to say a special word to women who have had an abortion. The Church is aware of the many factors which may have influenced your decision, and she does not doubt that in many cases it was a painful and even shattering decision. The wound in your heart may not yet have healed. Certainly what happened was and remains terribly wrong. But do not give in to discouragement and do not lose hope.

> — Pope John Paul II, *Evangelium Vitae (The Gospel of Life)*, 99

I have learned that the greatest power is hidden in patience. I see that patience always leads to victory, although not immediately; but that victory will become manifest after many years. Patience is linked to meekness.

— *Diary*, 1514

Patience

In spite of the fact that we feel remorse from our abortions, many of us, like the children of Israel, *complain against the Lord* when it comes to our healing.

If things are not going as fast as we would like, or if we still have moments of despair or struggle, we are quick to think that God is not there for us. We have no patience even though God has begun His work in us. When things are not going the way we think they should be, we grumble and think He has left us, instead of trusting in His love for us. We want healing *here* and *now*!

In the Gospels, Jesus makes a startling statement to the Pharisees: "For if you do not believe that I AM, you will die in your sins." He tells them that they will die, not because He cannot or would not save them, but because they did not believe in Him!

Today let us ask God to help us in our impatience, and to remind us that God is always in charge and that we need to trust the One who is the *I Am*.

"Consider it pure joy whenever you face trials of many kinds." "Patience," he explained, "has nothing to do with resignation, when we endure trials with faith they ripen our lives."

— Pope Francis, Homily, Domus Sanctae Marthae, February 17, 2014

Summer

Today I heard a voice in my soul: **Oh, if sinners knew my mercy, they would not perish in such great numbers. Tell sinful souls not to be afraid to approach Me; speak to them of my great mercy**.

— Diary, 1396

Turn Back the Hands of Time

There is an old song by R&B singer Tyrone Davis called, "Turn Back the Hands of Time." It is about a relationship, but I think if you passed the lyrics on to anyone who has had an abortion, they would be able to relate.

> *Can't sleep at night*
> *Always thinking about you*
> *But if I had the*
> *Chance to start all over*
> *I would be wishing today*
> *On a four leaf clover*
> *And leaving would be*
> *The last thing on my mind*
> *If I could turn back*
> *The hands of time*

The great deception of believing life will return to the way it was before abortion is still living and breathing among us. Often for women who are pregnant and feeling desperate, there is a great desire to trust that we can go ahead and abort without any repercussions. Only afterward do we discover that this is far from the truth.

Even the most staunch pro-choicer would admit to moments of melancholy after having had an abortion, if they are being honest. Even if they are adamant in believing they made the "right choice," there is still emptiness, and thoughts of birthdays missed and their child who is not there.

It would take a very cold heart to have an abortion that made no impact on you. Although those who say that they feel that way seem to brag as if that is a good thing, I would never want to be able to participate in the taking of the life of my child without it having any impact on me.

> *... can't hold out much longer*
> *Oh the pain's so deep and the hurt is getting stronger*
> *But if I had just one more try ... If I could turn*
> *back the hands of time ...*

We post-abortive parents may not be able to "turn back the hands of time," but we can move ahead to healing and wholeness. We can reclaim our children on a spiritual level, answering God's desire to give them to us. We can accept His forgiveness and His love in humility, and we can and should forgive ourselves.

If we truly turn ourselves over to Him and faithfully work through our healing, we will come to know that maybe we cannot turn back the hands of time, but we can look forward to the future when we will share eternity with our children and with God who is Mercy Himself!

> Lord, You are here, among us. Fix your gaze on me and tell me what I must do: how I must repent for my mistakes, my sins; what courage do I need to go forward on the path that You first created.
>
> — Pope Francis, Homily, May 22, 2015

This Bread of the Strong gives me all the strength
I need to carry on my mission and the courage to
do whatever the Lord asks of me. The courage and
strength that are in me are not of me, but of Him
who lives in me — it is the Eucharist.

— Diary, 91

Beneath the Veil of Holy Bread

Beneath the veil of Holy Bread
My Savior comes to me
He calls me to His perfect love
And all I'm meant to be

He pushes through my many fears
To show me He is there
And in those times of deepest pain
With me the Cross He'll bear

Mary guides me on the way
Encouragement she gives
She's trodden down this path herself
And knows that Jesus lives

A call to deep abandonment
And trust beyond compare
She tells me when I reach the end
They'll all be standing there

But in this present moment
He is alive as well
Our meeting in the Eucharist
His life in me to dwell
And through this veil of living bread
My son I get to feel

Until my journey comes to end
And God lifts up the veil.

> Help us, Jesus, to understand that in order "to do"
> in your Church, also in the field of the new evange-
> lization that is so urgently needed, we must first
> learn "to be," that is, to stay with you, in your sweet
> company, in adoration. Authentic, effective and
> true apostolic action can only come from intimate
> communion with you.
>
> — Pope John Paul II, To the young people of Rome
> and Lazio gathered for Eucharistic Adoration,
> Basilica of St. John Lateran, March 15, 2005

I demand from you deeds of mercy, which are to arise out of love for Me. You are to show mercy to your neighbors always and everywhere. You must not shrink from this or try to excuse or absolve yourself from it.

— Diary, 742

You Shall Love Your Neighbor

I have often thought if we do not love ourselves, we cannot love our neighbors. I'm not saying we need selfish love, but rather God's self-giving love.

If we are living sinful lives and do not have the life of Christ in us, it will become evident in our relationships with others. We cannot give what we do not have.

We also cannot love God the way we should unless we first really know Him and His love for us. It is through knowing this love that we are then able to grow in love and love Him as we should. Only His love allows us to do this.

Most people who come forward for healing from abortion are filled with self-loathing. They cannot even begin to look at their abortion experience until they first begin to know and experience the love of God for them. It is only through the light of trust in that love, a love often manifested through others, that post-abortive people feel safe enough to examine such a horrific act. It is the means to heal and to forgive themselves and others who may have been involved. Then they are able to freely love their neighbor.

May each of us who have experienced the mercy of Christ show that same mercy to others, so that they, too, may love as Christ does.

> Today's Gospel reminds us that the whole law of God is summed up in love for God and neighbor ... You cannot love God without loving your neighbor and you cannot love your neighbor without loving God.
>
> — Pope Francis, *Angelus*, October 28, 2014

My daughter, know that My Heart is mercy itself. From this sea of mercy, graces flow out upon the whole world. No soul that has approached Me has ever gone away unconsoled. All misery gets buried in the depths of My mercy, and every saving and sanctifying grace flows from this fountain.

— *Diary*, 1777

Faith Out of Desperation

In the Gospel, we read about the royal official who went to Jesus because his son was ill and near death (see Jn 4:49). Although he did not know Jesus, he seemed to believe that if he asked, Jesus was sure to heal his son. Who knows what he had heard about Him? I imagine that he had heard about many healings that had already taken place. It always amazed me that this official had so much faith.

Upon more thought, however, I wondered if the official went to Jesus, not out of faith, but out of desperation. Maybe he knew his son was going to die, and this was the only hope he had of a possible cure.

I did not go to Jesus for my healing out of faith; I went out of desperation. I had tried everything in order to forget and move on with my life, but there was no moving on; there was no forgetting. Jesus was my last hope. I felt I had nothing to lose. Things couldn't get any worse than they already were, so why not try Him? I guess you would call it hitting rock bottom. I knew I could not do it. I knew I needed help, so what the heck. What did I have to lose?

The official made the decision to believe out of love for his son. His son brought him to a relationship with God. My aborted son, Joshua, did the same for me.

It does not matter what our motivation is for seeking God. Most people seek Him because they know in their hearts something is missing.

As St. Augustine said, "God, you have made us for yourself, and *our hearts are restless* till they find their rest in you."

> Where if not in the Divine Mercy can the world find refuge and the light of hope?
>
> — Pope John Paul II, Homily, Beatification of Sr. Faustina, April 18, 1993

Jesus: **My daughter, do you think you have written enough about My mercy? What you have written is but a drop compared to the ocean. I am Love and Mercy Itself. There is no misery that could be a match for My mercy, neither will misery exhaust it, because as it is being granted — it increases. The soul that trusts in My mercy is most fortunate, because I Myself take care of it**.

— Diary, 1273

His Mercy Endures Forever

The parable of the Prodigal Son (see Lk 15:11-32) is one of my favorite scriptures. I love the humanness of all the characters Jesus describes and how God expresses His love for each one of them, wherever they may be on their journey to Him.

I also can personally relate to each one of the characters in the parable. Perhaps that was His intention, that we all may recognize that we have a little of each one of them in us.

The most obvious connection for me, of course, in light of my abortion is the son who took his wealth, went off, and squandered it all on crazy living. He returns home only after he has realized that pigs have a better life then he does, and all his high living has brought him to naught.

Of course, the most wonderful part of the story is that his father not only accepts him back, but also runs out to greet him, kills the fatted calf, and celebrates the return of his lost son. He does not sit the prodigal son down and throw everything back in his face. The father does not scold him or shame him. He embraces the younger son and calls for a celebration to mark his return to the fold, much as God does when we return to Him after abortion.

If you are new to the healing process and still worry about how you'll be received by God after you've had an abortion, read the story of the Prodigal Son and talk to someone who has made the journey back into the fold after an abortion before you. I can assure you, God's mercy endures forever.

> Indeed, mercy is the central nucleus of the Gospel message; it is the very name of God, the Face with which he revealed himself in the Old Covenant and fully in Jesus Christ, the incarnation of creative and redemptive Love. May this merciful love also shine on the face of the Church and show itself through the sacraments, in particular that of Reconciliation, and in works of charity, both communitarian and individual. May all that the Church says and does manifest the mercy God feels for man, and therefore for us. When the Church has to recall an unrecognized truth or a betrayed good, she always does so impelled by merciful love, so that men and women may have life and have it abundantly.
>
> — Pope Benedict XVI, *Regina Caeli*,
> Castel Gandolfo, March 30, 2008

Let no soul fear to draw near to Me, even though its sins be as scarlet.

— *Diary*, 699

Be Merciful to Me, a Sinner

There are some ways in which I can see how God has brought good out of the evil of my abortion. Probably the most evident good is my knowledge that I am a sinner. There is no denying that, and no way to get around it. The fact that I killed my unborn child is there each day, forcing me to acknowledge that I am a sinner.

I don't find myself saying, "How could this person have done this or that?" I truly understand how someone can get caught up in something and sin, no matter how horrible the sin. For this knowledge, I am grateful.

This, of course, does not mean I am glad I had an abortion. Of course not! But it does mean I am aware of my sinfulness and how much I need God's mercy in my life. It means that I know that if I stray from His teachings, it will not be long before I am out there doing the same sinful things that I used to do and hurting myself and others gravely.

For me, it is a relief to know myself. That was not always so. There was a time in my life when it terrified me to see my sins. I am not saying I enjoy seeing my faults, but when I do, I throw myself on God's mercy, trusting in Him instead of myself. I know He will not let me down, and it is in this that I find my peace.

This is me, a sinner on whom the Lord has turned his gaze. And this is what I said when they asked me if I would accept my election as pontiff. I am a sinner, but I trust in the infinite mercy and patience of our Lord Jesus Christ, and I accept in a spirit of penance.

— Pope Francis, interview,
America Magazine, Sept. 30, 2013

Know that by fighting bravely you give Me great glory and amass merits for yourself. Temptation gives you a chance to show Me your fidelity. … [Saint Faustina wrote:] Each battle valiantly fought brings me joy, peace, light, experience and courage for the future; honor and glory to God; and in the end, for me, a reward.

— *Diary*, 1560, 499

Spiritual Flip-Flops

I am known as the flip-flop girl. My friends joke, "You know when it's snowing because Theresa doesn't have her flip-flops on!" As true as that is, in the spiritual life, I definitely wear running shoes!

I do not like to feel emptiness or pain. My human nature completely rebels against it. As much as I hate to admit it, I am smitten with myself, in spite of the fact that I know I am my own worst enemy.

As soon as I feel that emptiness, I begin running to fill it up with something — most times one of my many vices — determined to do anything to avoid experiencing the void. I busy myself with trivial things; I run around; I feed my emotions with a variety of distractions, from food to other means of entertainment. Most times I do everything but what I know I should be doing: praying, sitting in silence, and allowing myself to experience that emptiness so that the only One who truly can fill it can find a place to reside. I forget that He is right here wherever I am, ready to help me.

I know I am not alone in this behavior. None of us likes emptiness and pain. The pain of a past abortion often leads people into all kinds of negative behaviors, including drug addictions, eating disorders, or sexual addictions — anything to avoid thinking about the reality of what we did.

It is such a paradox because once we learn to deal with these feelings with the help of those who know the dynamics of abortion (the ways it affects your life); once we allow ourselves to sit still in the pain and emptiness; once we allow ourselves to mourn the loss of our children (and probably many other things) and work through our issues, we come to experience His love and peace. Instead of suffering the bondage that behaviors of avoidance can bring us, we can sift through the pain and emptiness little by little. We can choose to look for and trust in God in the midst of the void, where we are sure to find Him walking on the road with us, waiting to forgive and heal us.

It's funny: No matter how many times I have found this to be true, I still find myself scampering around, running to fill any void I am feeling. It may not be the void of abortion anymore, but I still have to stop, catch myself, and pull myself back to the truth of who I am and the truth of who He is; the truth of my need for Him; the truth that He knows better than I do what is good for me; and the truth that His love and mercy are always there for me.

So I may still run, but by His grace, before I get too far down the road, I now change to my spiritual flip-flops and walk hand in hand with the One who heals me.

> Even Christians run away from God.
>
> — Pope Francis, Homily, Domus Sanctae Marthae,
> October 7, 2013

Although the desert is fearful, I walk with lifted head and eyes fixed on the sun: that is to say, on the merciful Heart of Jesus!

— *Diary*, 886

Trusting in the Midst of Fear

In my talks, I often speak of how shy I was before my healing. I make a joke of it, but it is completely true: I was afraid to order McDonald's. That is how timid I was. Now, God has me speaking publicly of my worst sin, often in front of thousands of people! Talk about the transforming power of the Holy Spirit!

I have come to disassociate myself from my talks in my own mind because I truly believe they are about Jesus and what He has done in my life, not about me and what I have done. The miracle of my healing has given me the great gift of courage through my faith, something I am so grateful for and without which I would not be able to do this work. It has also given me great freedom, because my trust is in Him, not in myself. Before every talk, I ask Him to kick me out of the way and give me the words He would have me say.

Does this mean there is never any anxiety or fear? Of course not! However, those anxious or fearful times are the times where I allow it to be about me instead of about Him, when my human nature is fighting to take over and either get me to quit or get me to fumble. Sometimes, I am tormented for days before a talk, and it is only my faith in Him that allows me to continue.

I move forward in spite of the fear because I know it is His will for me. I may have to drag myself to the place I am to speak, fighting myself all the way, but the important thing is that I go, in spite of all I am feeling.

I am sure that a part of Jesus wanted to run the other way many times during His ministry, especially on the way to Golgotha, but He also knew the goodness and love of the Father and what He willed for the Son, and trusted in that goodness.

So, I drag myself along. I pray to kick myself out of the way, keep my eyes on Him, and trust that He will provide what it is I am meant to say. I ask for Our Lady's inter-cession, as always, and I speak to the truth of abortion, its destruction of the unborn, and its damage to countless others. Then I watch the grace of God work as He touches hearts and minds with His mercy.

> Have no fear of entrusting yourselves to him! He will guide you, he will grant you the strength to follow him every day and in every situation.
>
> — Pope John Paul II, 15th World Youth Day, Vigil of Prayer, Tor Vergata, August 19, 2000

Jesus: **Be not afraid of your Savior, O sinful soul. I make the first move to come to you, for I know that by yourself you are unable to lift yourself to me. Child, do not run away from your Father; be willing to talk openly with your God of mercy who wants to speak words of pardon and lavish his graces on you. How dear your soul is to Me! I have inscribed your name upon My hand; you are engraved as a deep wound in My Heart.**

— Diary, 1485

Need of Mercy

I love the Gospel reading of the woman caught in adultery (see Jn 8:1-11). It is not surprising since, as post-abortive people, we all can relate to her. I am sure her feelings were very much the same as the ones we have experienced: guilt, shame, confusion, anxiety, or fear of condemnation. I am sure she felt like the worst sinner in the world.

But Jesus did not condemn her. Instead, we are told, He did not even look at her; *He bent over and wrote on the ground with His finger.* I often think of how He did this so that she would not feel ashamed or embarrassed. He did not want to increase her anxiety and fear, but instead wanted to invite her to trust in His mercy.

Unlike Jesus, the people around her were condemning her. They had picked up their stones, ready to put her to death, but Jesus, knowing the sinfulness of every person, changed the course of events. "Let the one among you who is without sin be the first to throw a stone at her" (Jn 8:7).

This was a call for them to look at their own lives instead of judging hers. One by one, they left, aware of their own sinfulness, aware that each of us needs the mercy of God.

"Neither do I condemn you. Go, [and] from now on do not sin anymore" (Jn 8:11). I know what that woman felt like. She experienced overwhelming gratitude for the forgiveness and mercy of God, but also a call to amend her life, a call to change her ways so that she would not sin again, so she would not hurt others or herself. She felt a challenge to grow in true love: the love of God. May we sin no more, by His grace, and invite others to the same mercy He has shown to us.

> We look at the sky, there are many, many stars; but when the sun rises in the morning, the light is such that we can't see the stars. God's mercy is like that: a great light of love and tenderness. God forgives us, not with a decree, but with his love, healing the wounds of sin. Because He is involved in forgiveness, He is involved in our salvation. So when Jesus acts as confessor to the woman he does not humiliate her, he does not say: "What have you done? When did you do it? How did you do it? With whom did you do it?" No! He says: "Go and do not sin again!" God's mercy is great, Jesus's mercy is great. Forgive us and heal us!
>
> — Pope Francis, Homily, Vatican Radio, April 7, 2014

Do not fear, My little child, you are not alone. Fight bravely, because My arm is supporting you; fight for the salvation of souls, exhorting them to trust in My mercy, as that is your task in this life and in the life to come.

— *Diary*, 1452

Waiting for Prince Charming

I have to admit, doing post-abortive work in the pro-life movement often leaves me feeling like a stepchild longing for the appearance of Prince Charming, that perfect person to sweep me off my feet and provide for the needs of the ministry.

As the ministry grows, so do its needs. It is a good problem, but nonetheless one that begs to be addressed.

"I have not come to call the righteous but sinners to repentance" (Lk 5:32).

Post-abortion ministry is one that calls sinners to repentance. It is a quiet call to Christ, who loves them in spite of their sins. It helps bring about the reunion of a creature with their Creator. People come to our ministry to learn of God's unfathomable love and mercy, which reunites them with their unborn children, bringing about the spiritual relationship that God had intended. Those who long for the healing touch of a loving God can find a richness of mercy in this ministry.

In the end, I have come to realize Prince Charming is already here. Instead of a castle, He was born in a stable.

Instead of a chariot, He rode on a donkey. Instead of praise, He received suffering, crucifixion, and death for our sins. We may not have all the material things we need or even the temporal support, but we have Him, the Prince of Peace, the King of Kings. Who needs anything more?

May He bring many souls back to His Heart and healing from the scourge of abortion that has touched our land, for it is in His Heart that our treasure lies.

> The kingdom of God makes itself present in the very person of Jesus. He is the hidden treasure and the pearl of great price. It encompasses the joy of the peasant and the merchant: they found it! It is the joy of all of us when we discover the closeness and the presence of Jesus in our lives — a presence that transforms our lives.
>
> — Pope Francis, Homily, Feast of St. Anne,
> July 26, 2014

He who knows how to forgive prepares for himself many graces from God. As often as I look upon the cross, so often will I forgive with all my heart.

— Diary, 390

You Are Loved

I have been blessed with some incredible friends, ones who have known me at my best and my worst, and still unconditionally love me. They have been with me through good times and bad. We have laughed, cried, rejoiced, and mourned together. I thank God for them always, and I pray they feel the same way about me.

A friendship like that is truly an amazing gift from God, one that challenges us to grow in love. We can be our true selves and know that our friend will still be there, loving us in spite of any failings. We know we are accepted as we are.

But I also know the pain of a relationship where the love only goes in one direction, a relationship that perhaps I think is one sort of connection, and then painfully come to discover that the other person has been thinking of it completely differently.

In these relationships, I would often accept unacceptable behavior because I did not want to see the truth. I would find a million excuses not to see the signs that were screaming out to me because I did not want to believe that the person I cared for so deeply did not feel the same way about me.

"It must have been a mistake."

"I am sure he/she did not realize how hurtful that was."

"I will tell them how hurt I felt, and surely it will not happen again."

But it always did. I would come up with a million excuses to avoid finally facing the fact that a person did not feel about me the same way I felt about them.

There was a time after my abortion when my self-esteem was so low that I saw every failed relationship as a reflection of my own worth. I believed I was unlovable, and so it was always my fault. How could someone love me, a mother who had taken the life of her child? Of course they would leave!

Over the years through my healing in Jesus Christ, I have come to learn it is not always about me. I am never alone or unloved. He is there with me through it all. It does not make the lesson any less painful, especially if you have given years of your life to a relationship. Clinging to unhealthy relationships and trying to force them to become something else, or to believe what you want instead of what is actually real, is not a good thing and destroys your peace of mind.

Of course, we are called to forgive, but forgiveness does not mean continuing to abide in an unhealthy relationship. It is painful to let go of something or someone we truly loved, but if we are honest with ourselves, we will come to realize that it is not good for either of us in the end.

Jesus, I trust in you!

Certainly, forgiveness does not come spontaneously or naturally to people. Forgiving from the heart can sometimes be actually heroic. The pain of losing a child, a brother or sister, one's parents or whole family as a result of war, terrorism or criminal acts can lead to the total closing of oneself to others. People who have been left with nothing because they have been deprived of their land and home, refugees and those who have endured the humiliation of violence, cannot fail to feel the temptation to hatred and revenge. Only the warmth of human relationships marked by respect, understanding and acceptance can help them to overcome such feelings. The liberating encounter with forgiveness, though fraught with difficulties, can be experienced even by a wounded heart, thanks to the healing power of love, which has its first source in God who is Love.

— Pope John Paul II, Celebration of the XXX World Day of Peace, January 1, 1997

At three o'clock, implore My mercy, especially for sinners; and, if only for a brief moment, immerse yourself in My Passion, particularly in My abandonment at the moment of agony. This is the hour of great mercy for the whole world. I will allow you to enter into My mortal sorrow. In this hour, I will refuse nothing to the soul that makes a request of Me in virtue of My Passion.

— Diary, 1320

Abandonment

How can you put into words the feeling of complete and total abandonment? How would you accurately convey a pain that reaches your very core, the deepest recesses of your soul?

Once that part of you has been touched, it is hard to forget it. There seems to always be a part of you attached to that pain, that cross that you carry, even though most times you may not feel the weight. Every once in a while, it rears its ugly head, projecting into the present what was so painful in the past. It can be hard to identify what is happening; you may even find yourself sabotaging relationships to spare yourself from being abandoned again.

Many post-abortive people have abandonment issues. Often they were abandoned at the time of their abortion by boyfriends, husbands, or parents who loved them — but not enough, in their human weakness, to help those women who were contemplating abortion to give life to their child. What a choice to have to make! Do you choose the love of those whom you believe care for you or your child whom you have not yet met? Coerced into abortion out of fear of abandonment or actually abandoned by your loved ones in order to coerce you to abort — it makes no difference: The results are the same.

I think back over the years, seeing how many times this abortion "connector" (people, places, or things that trigger the memory of your abortion experience) of abandonment defined moments in my life before I understood what was happening. My struggles with abandonment still pop up, and I am sure always will until the day I die. Even though it may take me awhile, I am always able to identify what is really happening and, by the grace of God, I talk myself back into the present moment instead of reacting to the past.

Surely, the sin I committed was great, but through my healing process, I have come to know Jesus Christ, who suffered abandonment freely for me. I meet Jesus every time I am connected with that pain in the present. He reminds me I am not alone and that we will walk through this together. Jesus touches me with His mercy, His love, His forgiveness, His clear view of the entire abortion, and His understanding. Not to say it was right — abortion is never right — but He loves me in spite of it.

I am a sinner in need of God's mercy. All good I do comes from Him; I can do nothing without Him. I do not heal people — He does; I do not save women from abortion — He does; I do not close abortion clinics — He does, and He is the only one who can do any of those things.

I pray for the humility to never forget that I am nothing without Him; to be grateful; to suffer willingly (even in the midst of dealing with the effects of my abortion connector that triggers a sense of abandonment) for the salvation of souls, knowing His great love for them and that He suffers with me; to always stay under the mantle of Our Mother of Mercy who leads me always to her Son; and to trust and not fear our God of Mercy, He who was Himself abandoned so that we could find Him.

> Faith itself enters into crisis because of negative experiences that make us feel like we are abandoned by the Lord. But this road to Emmaus on which we travel can become a way of purification and maturation of our believing in God.
>
> — Pope Benedict XVI, *Angelus*, April 6, 2008

I desire trust from My creatures. Encourage souls to place great trust in My fathomless mercy. Let the weak, sinful soul have no fear to approach Me, for even if it had more sins than there are grains of sand in the world, all would be drowned in the unmeasurable depths of My mercy.

— *Diary*, 1059

Amazing Truth

When we look at our sinfulness, there is a temptation to get stuck there. We keep the focus on ourselves and beat ourselves up because of our misery. We get stuck in the "I cannot believe I had an abortion" mode. This, however, is false pride. Why should we be so shocked that we can commit such a sin? Once we turn from the will of God, any sin is possible.

We are asked to move beyond that self-centered focus, to focus on the Passion of Jesus and His ultimate sacrifice for our sins, even for our sin of abortion. It is a time to meditate on His great love for us.

As we come to know this love, we do not make sacrifices during Lent only because we are told to do so, but instead because we cannot help loving Him and wanting to return a sacrifice out of that love.

Today, take a few minutes to sit before a cross and repeat, "Jesus died on the Cross for my sins, even my sin of abortion."

It is an amazing truth about God's love for you!

For our sake, God became one of us, sharing our human existence to the fullest and giving us in exchange a share in his own divine life. This great mystery reveals the reality and depth of God's love for us. It also invites us to respond to him in a faith which accepts the truth of his word and shapes our daily lives.

— Pope Benedict XVI, General Audience,
January 9, 2013

Fall

Tell souls not to place within their own hearts obstacles to My mercy, which so greatly wants to act within them. My mercy works in all those hearts which open their doors to it. Both the sinner and the righteous person have need of My mercy. Conversion, as well as perseverance, is a grace of My mercy.

— *Diary*, 1577

Getting Out of Your Own Way

Sometimes we can be so stuck on our own pain from abortion that we become self-centered. We obsess over it, thinking about it 24/7. Everything speaks to us about abortion. We can go over things in our head a million times and fill our lives with "if onlys."

This constant focus on self is not only unhealthy, but also unhelpful. "Would haves," "could haves," "should haves," and "if onlys" will get you nowhere, and thinking about your abortion 24/7 will not make the pain leave any earlier. In fact, it will most likely make things worse.

Instead, find a ministry or therapist that can help you work through your abortion. Put your abortion(s) in a box except when you are in a place where you will actually get help. That help should include assistance with learning about the dynamics of abortion, spiritual support, and people willing to lend an ear who can help you understand what happened. Some people fear that this will mean you are forgetting your baby. That is not true. You will still be dealing with the abortion, but in a healthy way in an environment where you can get actual help and clarification instead of just tormenting yourself.

Matthew 25:31-46 speaks of helping others. Whenever you see yourself sinking into the habit of obsession, take your focus off yourself by doing something for someone else. Not only will it help the other person, but it will help you as well.

> Seeing with the eyes of Christ, I can give to others much more than their outward necessities; I can give them the look of love which they crave.
>
> — Pope Benedict XVI, *Deus Caritas Est* (*God Is Love*), Encyclical Letter, December 25, 2005

Jesus: **I am your strength, I will help you in the struggle.**

— Diary, 1485

'Be Still and Know that I am God'

I do not know about the rest of you, but I have a hard time staying still and accepting suffering. The inability to let go of things that I cannot control, failing to recognize that God is allowing them for a reason, has often hurt me more than the original suffering. I cling to my will instead of His. A part of me still seeks to act on my emotions or change a situation over which I truly have no power.

I am now more conscious of my mental and emotional patterns. I try not to act on my emotions, which often rage in times of deep hurt. Sometimes I succeed and sometimes I fail, but with the help of God, I am learning to "be still."

I have also learned that it is OK to lament to God who hears our prayers and sees the truth of any situation. That is why it was so nice to read Pope Francis' words: "lamenting suffering is a form of prayer and is not a sin" (Homily, Domus Sanctae Marthae, April 7, 2014).

Still, I must work at bringing my emotions to God. Then I need to "be still," trusting in Him and His love for me.

It is not easy letting go (something we often have to do to be still), especially of things close to our hearts. It is a struggle; it is dying to self, and some days it is easier than others, but when we do get the grace, it is totally freeing and allows us to cling to God alone, He who knows our hearts, loves us, and longs to fill us with His life.

Therefore, in the midst of suffering, although I may not "feel" it, I thank You, God, for this suffering with which I know you are purifying me and bringing me closer to Your Heart!

> A priest I know once said to a woman who lamented to God about her misfortune, "But, madam, that is a form of prayer; go ahead with it" … To lament before God is not a sin.
>
> — Pope Francis, Homily, Vatican Radio, June 5, 2013

Even if there were a sinner most hardened, if he were to recite this chaplet only once, he would receive grace from My infinite mercy. I desire that the whole world know My infinite mercy. I desire to grant unimaginable graces to those souls who trust in My mercy.

— *Diary*, 687

The Greatest Sinner

A few years ago, I got a phone call from a good friend of mine. Of course, she is privy to a lot that is going on in my life. She was hardly able to contain her laughter. She had seen an article from the 2009 North American Congress on Mercy in Washington, D.C., where I had spoken. "Boy," she exclaimed, "God certainly wants you to be humble!"

(If you have not seen the article, you can check it out in Part One.)

The article was titled, "'I Couldn't Fathom What I Had Done.' A Message for the Greatest Sinners." The metaphorical stamp is on my head; "guilty" says the sign on my back, and "she killed her child." Only the funny thing is, I did know what I had done. I didn't feel shame. I didn't feel insulted, I didn't feel embarrassed or like it was untrue. I was at peace with it.

Why? Because, through the Divine Mercy of God, I have found healing from those emotions of shame, embarrassment, and guilt. Instead of being afraid and running from what I had done, I can now openly confront the knowledge that I am a sinner, and while I strive not to sin, I am also aware that anything I do right is because of God's grace in my life.

The things I feared to face and deal with before my healing have become the things I am at peace with in the light of God's love and mercy and all that He has done for me. I now stand in truth, the truth of my sin and the truth of God's mercy. There is nowhere else I would rather be.

Because of this, I was able to join in the laughter with my good friend, not about my sin itself, but about the truth of myself, knowing that I am "the greatest sinner" and that God is the God of Mercy!

> I am a sinner, but I trust in the infinite mercy and patience of our Lord Jesus Christ, and I accept in a spirit of penance.
>
> — Pope Francis, "My Door is Always Open:
> Conversations of Faith, Hope and the Church
> in a Time of Change" with Antonio Spadaro,
> *America* Magazine, September 30, 2013

When I look into the future, I am frightened,
But why plunge into the future?
Only the present moment is precious to me,
As the future may never enter my soul at all.

It is no longer in my power,
To change, correct or add to the past,
For neither sages nor prophets could do that,
And so, what the past has embraced I must
    trust to God.

O present moment, you belong to me, whole
    and entire.

— *Diary*, 2

Embracing the Present

Those who have had an abortion can get stuck in the past.
They can spend their lives immersed in regret, playing the
same tired script a million times in their head: "I should
have … I could have … I cannot believe … ." Their lives are
stuck on the abortion experience.

While it is important to understand what has happened to
us and why things happened as they did, it is not useful or
healing to try to change what has already happened in our
heads. As St. Faustina says above, it is impossible.

Humbly accepting our failings and ability to sin, learning
from them, and trying to amend our lives in the present
moment are all we can do. Living God's will for us in the
present moment is where our healing takes place, right
here, right now!

I often pray to know and do God's will day by day, some-times minute by minute. Of course, I fail often, but my intentions are good, and I recognize that I am a sinner in need of His grace for all I do. Rather than imprisoning me, this knowledge frees me. I know that without Him, I can do nothing. So, I ask Him each day to live in me.

It is easy to keep the focus on ourselves when something so traumatic has happened to us. Pray for the grace to let go and focus on Him, instead. It is there you will find your peace.

> Without God man neither knows which way to go, nor even understands who he is ... One of the deepest forms of poverty a person can experi-ence is isolation ... Poverty is often produced by a rejection of God's love, by man's basic and tragic tendency to close in on himself, thinking himself to be self-sufficient or merely an insignificant and ephemeral fact, a "stranger" in a random universe ... The human being develops when ... his soul comes to know itself and the truths that God has implanted deep within, when he enters into dialogue with himself and his Creator ... It is not by isolation that man establishes his worth, but by placing himself in relation with others and with God.
>
> — Pope Benedict XVI, Encyclical Letter *Caritas in Veritate (In Charity and Truth)*, 78

O Jesus, You know how weak I am; be then ever with me; guide my actions and my whole being, You who are my very best Teacher! Truly, Jesus, I become frightened when I look at my own misery, but at the same time I am reassured by Your unfathomable mercy, which exceeds my misery by the measure of all eternity. This disposition of soul clothes me in Your power. O joy that flows from the knowledge of one's self! O unchanging Truth, Your constancy is everlasting!

— *Diary*, 66

Tenderness

There is an amazing thing about post-abortive healing: You do not have to do anything to earn it. It comes freely, which is hard to believe for those of us who participated in the death of our children.

The longing for forgiveness and acceptance can be huge after abortion. Feeling totally unforgiveable and lost, we often will do anything to feel accepted, to "make up" for our sin. The bad news is that there is nothing we can do to make up for our sin; the good news is that we do not have to because Jesus Christ already has by dying on the Cross.

One of my favorite parables is of the woman caught in adultery. She is dragged out before the public, who stand ready to condemn and stone her to death. Then Jesus speaks: "If any one of you is without sin, let him be the first to throw a stone at her" (Jn 8:3-8), and one by one, the crowd disperses.

Even more beautiful to me is the fact that Jesus is so conscious of her shame and guilt that He keeps His eyes on the ground because He does not want to add to her pain. His compassion for her suffering, even though it was a result of her sins, speaks to the depths of His mercy and love for her. "Woman, where are they? Has no one condemned you?" He asks; she replies, "No one, sir." Then Jesus says, "Neither do I condemn you. Go, [and] from now on do not sin anymore."

That is the forgiveness Jesus gives her, and that is the forgiveness He gives to those of us who are post-abortive. He does not tell us, "You are forgiven, but you must speak out about how terrible abortion is," or "You are forgiven, but you have to stand in front of a clinic and pray," or "You need to do 50 rosaries daily to make up for what you have done." No, He tells us as he told her, "Go and sin no more." Yes, we may do acts of reparation out of love for God and neighbor, or as a way to show gratitude for God's forgiveness. All that is good, but we can't "earn" love and forgiveness. Christ has given that freely.

Respect Life Month (October) can be very difficult for those who have had abortions. It can feel as if a neon light is shining on you for the entire month. Let's face it: The subject is everywhere. As we move through this month, let us always remember the tenderness of Jesus who did not shame the adulterous woman, but showed her unconditional love, a love that brought her into relationship with Him.

> We are all sinners, but God heals us with an abundance of grace, mercy and tenderness.
>
> — Pope Francis, @pontifex, Twitter,
> October 28, 2013, 7:15 AM

And Jesus said, **For you I am Mercy itself, therefore I ask you to offer Me your misery and this very helplessness of yours and, in this way, you will delight My Heart.**

— *Diary*, 1775

Trusting to the Point of Folly

Sanctity, as *Saint Thérèse* of Lisieux says, is expressed *most fully, not in actions* or specific deeds but in a disposition of the heart which makes us little and humble in the arms of Our Father, aware of our weakness and helplessness, yet trusting to the point of folly in his Fatherly love.

— S.C. Biela, *In the Arms of Mary*, page 74.

Sometimes it feels like God is pushing me more and more to deeper levels of trust. It is not easy. Life can be challenging. Sometimes it seems that, no matter where we look, there are issues to be dealt with, battles to be fought, work to be done, but mostly, practice in the art of letting go and trusting to the *point of folly*.

I have a special devotion to St. Thérèse. I was named after her because of my paternal grandfather's huge devotion to her. I am convinced she had more than a little to do with my conversion.

Aunt Lucy often told me how, for years, she prayed daily for St. Thérèse's intercession to bring me back to the faith. When I did return to the faith, *The Story of a Soul* (Thérèse's autobiography) was the first spiritual book I was given to read by a priest who was giving me spiritual direction.

In the midst of confronting my sinfulness and living in darkness and despair, the simple spirituality of St. Thérèse made conversion and even holiness seem attainable.

It was a relief to hear what I already knew: I could never do it on my own, so I needed to throw myself into our Father's arms with trust in His love for me. He would do the rest.

Saint Thérèse also gave me the tools to deal with the darkness that enveloped my life because of abortion. Those times when I felt immersed in a darkened tunnel, unable to see or feel any hope because of my grave sin, her words were more than a little comforting.

> O Jesus, Your little bird is happy to be weak and little. What would become of it if it were big? Never would it have the boldness to appear in Your presence, to fall asleep in front of You. Yes, this is still one of the weaknesses of the little bird: when it wants to fix its gaze upon the Divine Sun, and when the clouds prevent it from seeing a single ray of that Sun, in spite of itself, its little eyes close, its little head is hidden beneath its wing, and the poor little thing falls asleep, believing all the time that it is fixing its gaze upon its Dear Star. When it awakens, it doesn't feel desolate; its little heart is at peace and it begins once again its work of love. It calls upon the angels and saints who rise like eagles before the consuming Fire, and since this is the object of the little bird's desire the eagles take pity on it, protecting and defending it, and putting to flight at the same time the vultures who want to devour it. These vultures are the demons whom the little bird doesn't fear, for it is not destined to

be their prey but the prey of the Eagle whom it contemplates in the center of the Sun of Love.[*]

How often have I thought of that "little bird" and chosen to face the Divine Sun in spite of what I felt! Saint Thérèse made Heaven accessible to me. She was so human. She spoke of her "little way of confidence and love," trusting in His goodness to her to the point of folly.

Saint Thérèse made it possible for me to believe in healing, forgiveness, and mercy because she made me recognize that not only was I unable to do all these things for myself, but I did not need to. God wanted to bring me healing, forgiveness, and mercy because of His love for me, in spite of my failings and weaknesses.

Trusting to the point of folly is a road to sanctity, a road whose only requirement is a true act of the will to trust always in the One who came to give us life!

> The Psalmist begins by presenting God as a good shepherd who guides him to green pastures, standing at his side and protecting him from every danger. Such "green pastures" may seem distant to those who feel stranded in a spiritual desert, but if the Lord is the shepherd, even in the desert, a place of scarcity and death, we do not lose our certainty in the radical presence of life.
>
> — Pope Benedict XVI, General Audience,
> St. Peter's Square, May 10, 2011

[*] From *Story of a Soul*, translated by John Clarke, O.C.D. Copyright © 1975, 1976, 1996 by Washington Province of Discalced Carmelites ICS Publications 2131 Lincoln Road, N.E. Washington, DC 20002-1199 U.S.A. www.icspublications.org

Prayer to St. Faustina

O Jesus, who filled St. Faustina with profound
veneration for the boundless Divine Mercy, deign,
if it be Your holy will, to grant me through her
intercession, the grace for which I fervently pray.
My sins render me unworthy for Your mercy,
but be mindful of St. Faustina's sacrifice and
self-denial, and reward her virtues by granting
the petition, which, with childlike trust,
I present to You through her intercession.
Saint Faustina, pray for us.

Saint Faustina and Post-Abortion Healing

If I had to name one thing that was most instrumental
in my healing from abortion, it would be the devotion to
Divine Mercy. Anyone who has read my testimony (see
Part One) knows the role Divine Mercy has played in my
life. It was during hours of praying, "Jesus, I trust in You,"
that God chose to bring me onto His Cross and fill me with
His forgiveness and love. It was a personal crucifixion that
brought, not the pain we see as we gaze at the Cross, but a
flood of love that washed away my sin. So St. Faustina, of
course, holds a very special place in my heart.

This minister of mercy changed my life and brought me
hope. A person who thought there was no forgiveness for
her, a person so full of despair, was made to believe that, in
fact, God desired my healing and offered forgiveness.

While I lived under the guilt of my abortion, Faustina spoke to me through her *Diary* of Jesus' great desire to heal me through His mercy. "Divine Mercy In My Soul" spoke to *my* soul.

> Today, in the course of a long conversation, the Lord said to me, **How very much I desire the salvation of souls! My dearest secretary, write that I want to pour out My divine life into human souls and sanctify them, if only they were willing to accept My grace. The greatest sinners would achieve great sanctity, if only they would trust in My mercy** (*Diary*, 1784).

How could anyone refuse?

This devotion is still a major part of my life, and I am sure it always will be. It is the sure hope that allows me to do this work, because all my confidence is in His Mercy for every soul. The words, "Jesus, I trust in You," are my life-line — a confirmation that no matter what things look like, what life is handing out, or what I am feeling, *I only have to continue to trust*. I may only be able to do it for a minute, or perhaps just a second, but second by second, trust takes me through the trials of this life.

Knowing what God has done for me in freeing me from anxiety, fear, panic, depression — all the aftereffects of my abortion — gives me great confidence in Him in the midst of all that life brings. I know what He has done for me, and no one can take that away. It resides in a quiet place in my heart, guarded there from all that the outside world might bring.

It is this inner place of rest that allows me to do this work. It was this place that the *Entering Canaan* ministry was born from, and it is this place that sets my heart on fire to let others know of God's love, mercy, and forgiveness.

I believe in His Mercy because I know it is true! Jesus Christ freed me from the hell of abortion because He is Mercy!

Jesus, I trust in You!

> The Message of Divine Mercy has always been near and dear to me ... I took [it] with me to the See of Peter and [it] in a sense forms the image of this Pontificate.
>
> — Pope John Paul II, Address on his Pontificate, Shrine of Divine Mercy, Krakow, June 7, 1997

Before Holy Communion I saw the Blessed Mother inconceivably beautiful. Smiling at me She said to me, *My daughter, at God's command I am to be, in a special and exclusive way your Mother; but I desire that you, too, in a special way, be My child.*

— *Diary*, 1414

The Emptiness of Post-Abortion Healing

I do not think that anyone can really know what the emptiness of post-abortion healing feels like unless they experience that huge void in their heart, which becomes filled with feelings of guilt, shame, abandonment, and loneliness. I could go on and on, but if you are post-abortive, you know what it's like.

We also often try to fill it with unhealthy things like drugs, alcohol, eating disorders, and promiscuity. We somehow think that if we run fast enough, we can numb ourselves so that we will not notice the hole, but in the quiet of the night, we still feel its presence. Many times, that void gets filled with the spirit of depression, temptations to despair, or accusing screams telling us we're worthless and hopeless. But the truth is that there's always hope because Jesus Christ is our hope.

That being said, Jesus is not someone whom we can bargain with for our healing. We can't say, "If I do this or that, He will heal me." The feeling that I can somehow make up for what I have done if I could just do enough is a lie. Instead of being busy "doing," we need to get busy "being." We need to sit in the emptiness, knowing He has already made up for our abortions. We need to pray, not to ceaselessly attempt to make up for our sins, but to develop a relationship with God who loves us unconditionally and wants to heal us. We need to proclaim and trust in our healing and in our forgiveness (if we have been to the Sacrament of Reconciliation) because it really is there for us; Jesus died on the Cross for it. We need to sit still and listen to Him. In the end, God may call us to action, but it will be because we know His love and forgiveness, not to earn them, for they are freely given to those who feel contrition and confess.

We also need to obtain and learn about the tools we can't do without when we need to fight spiritual battles, feelings, and temptations to despair or believe we cannot be forgiven — feelings and temptations that are contrary to His will for us. These tools can be found through a good post-abortion ministry, a therapist knowledgeable in post-abortive healing, and most of all, others who have walked through the healing process before us. These relationships can help you in the battles that are sure to rage as you make your way to the Promised Land, to healing and restored relationships with God and your unborn child(ren). An army is always better than going solo. Others can watch your back to warn you of dangers and how to walk through them.

Plan your army, both spiritual and physical. Form your human army — people who can help you through the feelings and temptations when the battle is raging; people who are able to give you the weapons you need to silence the enemy; people who know the tactics used against us both by our own "stinking thinking" and on a spiritual level.

There is a beautiful line in the novena to "Our Lady, Undoer of Knots":

> *Come, dear Mother, not only to undo my knots, but to enter into the emptiness of my soul.*

Invite her into your emptiness where she will provide all that is needed through different avenues to bring you to the peace of her Son who died for your salvation.

> In the inner heart of every person the voice of God and the insidious voice of the Evil One can be heard. The latter seeks to deceive the human person, seducing him with the prospect of false goods, to lead him away from the real good that consists precisely in fulfilling the divine will.
>
> — Pope John Paul II, *Angelus*, March 9, 2003

Help me, O Lord, that my heart may be merciful so that I myself may feel all the sufferings of my neighbor. I will refuse my heart to no one. I will be sincere even with those who, I know, will abuse my kindness. And I will lock myself up in the most merciful Heart of Jesus. I will bear my own suffering in silence. May Your mercy, O Lord, rest upon me.

— *Diary*, 163

Healing Comes from Jesus Christ

It is not easy to heal from abortion. The very act of participating in the death of our children goes against everything nature has called us to be as mothers and fathers, that is, nurturers and protectors of the life created. The act of abortion touches us to our very core.

We can live in denial for a time, fighting within ourselves to justify and rationalize why we had abortions, but the truth is that nothing we can do could ever change the deep-rooted truth that we have taken the lives of our unborn children. Nothing can remove the guilt from that act or restore us to right relationship with God, our families and neighbors, our lost children, or even ourselves, except accepting and believing in the love and forgiveness of Jesus Christ.

I always tell those who come to the *Entering Canaan* ministry that healing is not a one-step process. Many times a post-abortive woman will come looking for a quick fix, for instant healing, but healing occurs in God's time, not ours. It is most often like peeling an onion, a process that involves working through many layers of issues, and the abortion itself is most often merely the culminating issue. There will be times when you will even feel like you are going backwards, but if you persevere and keep your eyes on Christ, healing will happen.

I remember one woman in particular who had had multiple abortions. When she came to us, she was in total despair. How could God ever forgive her? She believed she was the worst of the worst. No one had forced her to abort; she had freely chosen to end her pregnancies — or so she thought.

Each bit of progress in her healing was followed by bouts of despair, as the voice of condemnation began accusing her again, telling her forgiveness could never be hers. It often felt like she would take two steps forward and 10 steps backwards. She had to learn that healing was not about feelings, that she had to look at Jesus instead of herself, and that, in fact, she was making great progress in spite of what she felt. Now, years later, she is an amazing speaker. Although she does not publicly share her testimony out of consideration for her living children, she gives talks at our retreats, helping many other women on their healing journeys.

> The Christian must be a shining person, who brings light, who always gives light! A light that is not his, but a gift from God, it is Jesus' gift. And we carry this light.
>
> — Pope Francis, Address to World Day of the Sick and Winter Olympics Participants, February 10, 2014

I want to be completely transformed into Your mercy and to be Your living reflection, O Lord. May the greatest of all divine attributes, that of Your unfathomable mercy, pass through my heart and soul to my neighbor.

— *Diary*, 163

Be Merciful Just as Your Father is Merciful

It can be so hard to forgive and show mercy if we were coerced into having an abortion or if those around us did not support us when we were confronted with such a terrible decision. Just as we often feel we can never be forgiven, we also may feel like we cannot forgive the people who abandoned us or forced us to abort our unborn children. We think, "How can anyone expect us to do that?"

Yet that is exactly what God asks us to do. He commands us to forgive those who "trespass against us."

I remember how hard it was for me to forgive my dad who pressured me into having an abortion as a teen. I had to make up my mind that I was going to do it, to forgive him, and not once, but over and over and over again. I had to show him the mercy that God had shown me. Chances are that my unforgiveness never really affected my dad, but it tormented me because it separated me from God's peace.

Forgiving him was not easy, I admit, and without constant prayer and the grace of God, it was impossible for a while before I came to know Him again. But with His help, in time, I was able to forgive, and that forgiveness gave me peace because I was doing God's will.

In time, as my relationship with God grew, I learned to feel sorrow for my dad instead of anger at him. I learned to show him the mercy God had shown me, instead of judging him. It took years, but it happened, and in the end, God allowed me to be an instrument — through my forgiveness, not my anger — to bring my dad back to Him.

> It is not easy to love with a deep love, which lies in the authentic gift of self. This love can only be learned by penetrating the mystery of God's love. Looking at him, being one with his fatherly heart, we are able to look with new eyes at our brothers and sisters, with an attitude of unselfishness and solidarity, of generosity and forgiveness. All this is mercy!
>
> — Pope John Paul II, Homily,
> Canonization of St. Faustina, April 30, 2000

Let go of yourself, and abide with Me continually. Entrust everything to Me and do nothing on your own, and you will always have great freedom of spirit.

— *Diary*, 1685

Healing Families

There is no doubt that sin — all sin — touches each and every one of us. As a mother or father who has had an abortion, we often do not want to think of the pain that our decision to abort may cause our living children. We may even go so far as to deny that there will be any impact at all, as if learning of an aborted sibling would not have a negative impact.

I am not going to get into the question of whether someone should tell his or her children or not. That is a very personal decision. The answer may vary from person to person and family to family, and needs to be made after you have sought good counsel and spiritual direction. Instead, I am just going to mention a few things.

It is painful and hard to look at the result of abortion, but this, too, can be healed through God's mercy and good direction, whether it comes from a priest or counselor! It will take time, for sure, but in the end, God will use the truth of your abortion to bring your family even closer together if it is His will for you to tell your children, and even if you discern He is not calling you to tell them.

The road to healing is difficult for the siblings of a lost child, a road layered with the confusion of many emotions and consequences. They may ask questions like, "How could the people who are supposed to protect me kill my sibling? Where do I go with my pain? My feelings? Would I even be here if my sibling had not been aborted? Would my name be the same?" I could go on and on.

If I could say one thing to them, it would be, "Your life has dignity and worth, just as much dignity and worth as your sibling's. It was not your fault. Trust in our God of Mercy to heal you through and through. He does it. I have seen it time and again."

The scourge of abortion has touched our land, but so has the Blood of Christ, which cleanses and is greater than any sin.

> Sacred Scripture speaks to us of this reconciliation, inviting us to make every effort to attain it. But Scripture also tells us that it is above all a merciful gift of God to humanity. The history of salvation — the salvation of the whole of humanity as well as of every human being of whatever period — is the wonderful history of a reconciliation: the reconciliation whereby God, as Father, in the blood and the cross of his Son made man, reconciles the world to himself and thus brings into being a new family of those who have been reconciled.
>
> — Pope John Paul II, Apostolic Exhortation
> *On Reconciliation and Penance*,
> December 2, 1984

Do not bargain with any temptation; lock yourself immediately in My Heart and, at the first opportunity, reveal the temptation to the confessor. ... **Do not fear struggle; courage itself often intimidates temptations, and they dare not attack us.**

— *Diary*, 1760

Fighting Despair

I do not think there is one person who is reading this who has experienced abortion and would not relate to the following quote from Mother Teresa:

> The devil may try to use hurts of life, sometimes our own mistakes, to make you feel it is impossible that Jesus really loves you, is really cleaving to you. This is a danger for all of us. And so sad because it is completely opposite of what Jesus is really wanting, waiting to tell you ... He loves you always, even when you do not feel worthy.

When I first read this, I found it so reflective of the way the devil tempts those who have experienced abortion to despair. He comes whispering in our ear, that nagging voice encouraging us to lose hope for forgiveness, that murmuring that assails us so often before we have reached healing.

What a comfort to see that Mother Teresa had these same temptations to despair, and yet, in spite of what she may have felt, she knew Jesus loved her and loves us all!

Healing from an abortion has many aspects: emotional, spiritual, and sometimes physical. The devil wants nothing more than to make us despair of the Mercy of God, but God Himself reassures us.

The next time the devil tempts you and has you feeling unforgivable and unlovable, remember Mother Teresa's words and the truth about God's love for you!

> Jesus goes out of His way to offer despairing souls at death a final grace of repentance. When we know of souls that may be in spiritual peril, especially the dying, we should pray that they would respond to this grace of repentance.
>
> — Pope Benedict XVI, General Audience,
> October 18, 2006

Theresa Bonopartis

Theresa is the co-developer with the Sisters of Life of *Entering Canaan — a Sacramental Journey to an Inheritance of Mercy*, a post-abortion ministry program published by the United States Conference of Catholic Bishops, which consists of day retreats, weekend events, monthly gatherings, and special retreats.

In addition to the *Entering Canaan* women's ministry, she has also developed specialized days with the Franciscan Friars of the Renewal for men, siblings of aborted babies, and those who aborted as a result of an adverse diagnosis.

Having experienced abortion herself, her journey of healing has inspired many works across the world, including "An Afternoon of Prayerful Remembrance and Intercession," a prayer service she developed with the Family Life Office of New York, which has been televised by EWTN and conducted by many dioceses across the country.

In 2001, Reclaiming Our Children (ROC), of which Theresa is president, was formed and incorporated as the lay apostolate of the *Entering Canaan* ministry.

In June 2002, Theresa was the recipient of the second annual John Cardinal O'Connor Award for her work with those who are post-abortive. She currently is a member of the American Association of Christian Counselors, Post-Abortion Division, and also serves on the advisory board of Be Not Afraid, a ministry for those who have received an adverse pregnancy diagnosis.

Theresa's articles on healing can be found in many publications, including *Aleteia*, *Catholic Online*, *Catholic Exchange*, the *National Catholic Register*, *The Post Abortion Review*, and others. She can be seen in segments of EWTN's Sunday Night Prime speaking of healing, and has shared her story over the radio.

She currently is the director of Lumina/Hope & Healing after Abortion, a program of Good Counsel Homes (www.postabortionhelp.org).

Her great devotion to Divine Mercy (which was instrumental in her own healing journey) and Our Lady of Czestochowa, patroness of all her work, is the inspiration for all she does.

Theresa Bonopartis
Email: journeytohealingdm@gmail.com

Theresa currently blogs at:
www.reclaimingourchildren.typepad.com.

Jesus, we trust in You!
Our Lady of Czestochowa, pray for us!

Join the

Association of Marian Helpers,

headquartered at the National Shrine of The Divine Mercy, and share in special blessings!

**An invitation from
Fr. Joseph, MIC, the director**

Marian Helpers is an Association of Christian faithful of the Congregation of Marian Fathers of the Immaculate Conception.

By becoming a member, you share in the spiritual benefits of the daily Masses, prayers, and good works of the Marian priests and brothers. This is a special offer of grace given to you by the Church through the Marian Fathers.

Please consider this opportunity to share in these blessings, along with others whom you would wish to join into this spiritual communion.

Enroll Loved Ones

Give a Consoling Gift: *Prayer*

Enroll your loved ones in the Association of Marian Helpers, and they will be remembered in the daily Masses, prayers, good works, and merits of the Marian priests and brothers around the world.

Request a Mass
to be offered by the Marian Fathers for your loved one:

Individual Masses
(for the living or deceased)

Gregorian Masses
(30 days of consecutive Masses for the deceased)

1-800-462-7426
marian.org/enrollments   marian.org/mass